ADVANCED EXCEL FOR ACCOUNTANTS
PIVOT TABLES & VLOOKUP

THE ACCOUNTANTS GUIDE TO MASTERING PIVOT TABLES & VLOOKUP

Sterling Libs

Level 33, 25 Canada Square,

Canary Wharf, London E14 5LQ

resource@sterlinglibs.com

www.sterlinglibs.com

Straight Street Publishing

Editions ISBNs

Softcover

978-1-911037-08-8

i

Contents

Note to the reader

Pivot tables allow you to quickly summarize and analyse large amounts of data in lists and tables - independent of the original data layout in your spreadsheet - by dragging and dropping columns to different rows, columns, or summary positions.

Creating neat, informative summaries out of huge lists of raw data is a common challenge. And while Excel gives you all the tools you need to create such summaries, the actual work of writing formulas, cutting and pasting information, and organising your totals into a new table can be extremely tedious. Even worse, this approach isn't very flexible. For example, once you've created the perfect summary that compares, say, sales in different regions, if you want to compare sales across different product lines or different customers, you'll need to start from scratch and build a whole new report.

Fortunately, Excel has a feature called pivot tables that can solve all these problems. Pivot tables quickly summarise long lists of data. By using a pivot table, you can calculate summary information without writing a single formula or copying a single cell. But the most notable feature of pivot tables is that you can arrange them dynamically. For example, say you create a pivot table summary using raw census data. With the drag of a mouse, you can easily rearrange the pivot table so that it summarises the data based on gender or age groupings or geographic location. This process of rearranging your table is known as pivoting your data: you're turning the same information around to examine it from different angles.

In its most common usage, VLOOKUP is a database function, meaning that it works with database tables – or more simply, lists of things in an Excel worksheet. What sort of things? Well, any sort of thing. You may have a worksheet that contains a list of employees, or products, or customers, or CDs in your CD collection, or stars in the night sky. It doesn't really matter.

You are just about to get empowered with a complete mastery of this essential Excel tool.

I really look forward to walking you through the steps you need to once and for all get pivot tables and VLOOKUP as easy as possible for you.

Introduction

In the workplace, Excel is one of the most commonly used analysis and reporting tools.

Financial statements, sales reports, inventory, breakeven analysis, ratio analysis, monthly cash flow forecasts, operational budgets, customer activity – so much of this stuff is kept in Excel. Excel's ability to manipulate and give feedback about data makes it attractive. Accountants especially, can leverage on the powerful and complex features of Excel to streamline their work, save time and be more productive.

This step by step guide for Pivot Tables & VLOOKUP will enable you to master Excel's powerful and dynamic functions relevant to you as an accountant.

This book is about helping you produce financial reports quickly, accurately and systematically from a data base. Formulas are the keystone to analysing data – that is digging out nuggets of important information. Every Accountant should be able to analyse data and make sense of it especially when presenting financial reports to management and stakeholders.

The approach in this book uses a teaching technique that enables you to master the most fundamental features of Pivot Tables & VLOOKUP relevant to your role as an accountant and you will be able to do that in a fraction of the time needed when learning from conventional text books. Here are some of the unique features of this book:

- *The steps are carefully structured with screenshots & illustrations.*
- *Skills taught in the context of real accounting and business problems.*
- *The layout is presented on a one to one basis. It's like being walked through the steps by the best instructor.*
- *The presentation style allows you to learn only the skills that are essential to you as an accountant.*
- *There is a practical hands-on involvement*

Getting Started

In order to master this course, we are going to use business sample data/files to understand the powerful and complex functions and formulas in Excel. These sample files will be provided to you.

Excel Version

This practical guide is based on Excel 2013 Microsoft windows 8 operating system. You'll discover how to confirm that your computer is running in these version in a few minutes.

If you are using an earlier operating system (for example windows XP) this practical course will be equally relevant, but you may notice small differences in the appearance of some of the screenshots you will see in this practical guide.

This practical guide is written purely for Excel 2013 and, due to huge changes in this version, will not be useful for earlier versions (97, 2000, 2002 and 2003).

Checking your program and operating system

- *Start/open Excel on your computer.*

- *Click the "FILE" button at the top left corner as illustrated in the figure below.*

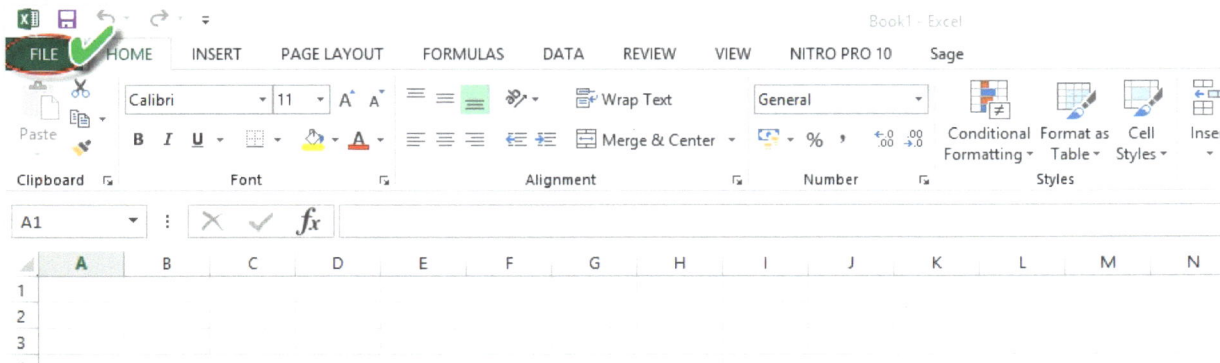

Fig. 1

- *After following the instructions above, a window similar to the figure below will appear.*

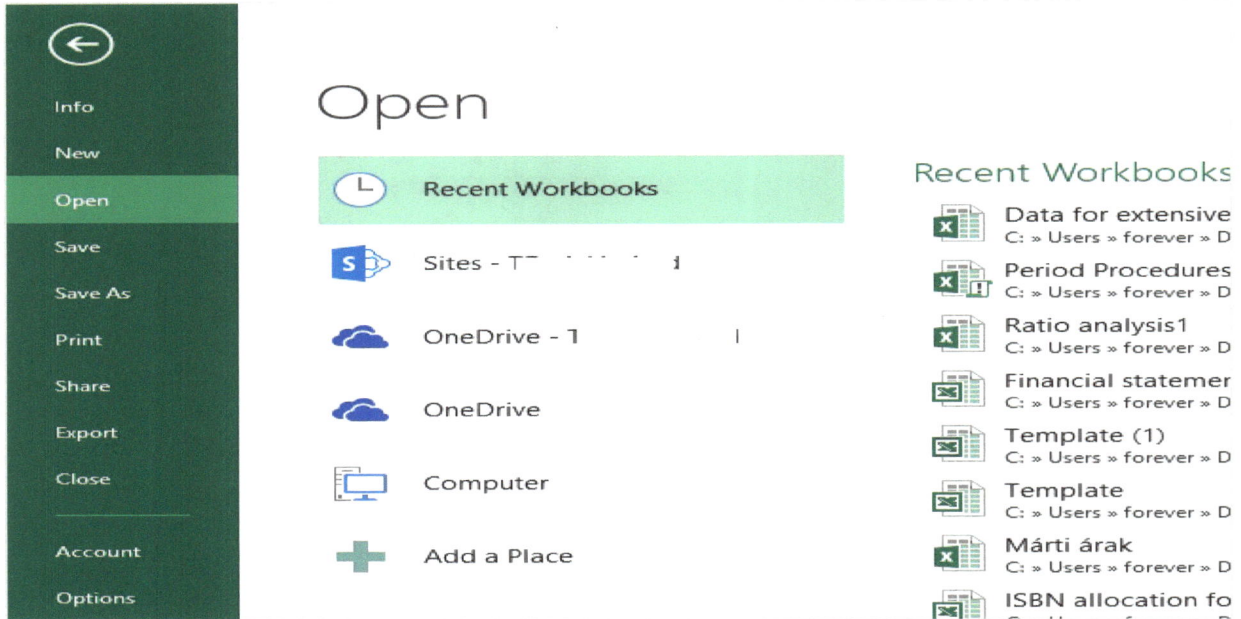

Fig. 2

- *Follow the instructions illustrated in the figure below.*

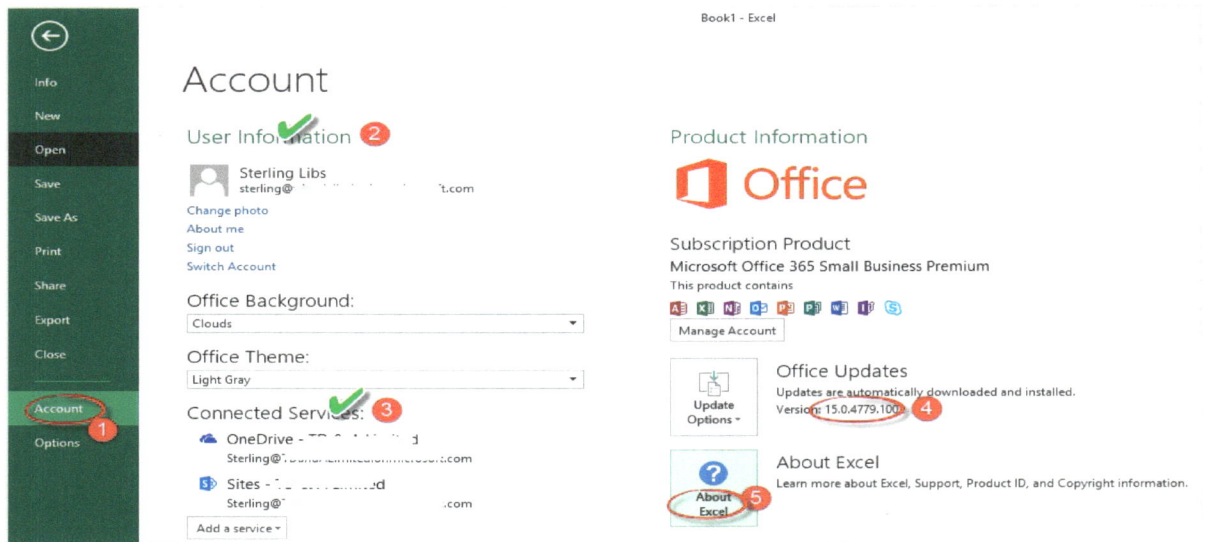

Fig. 3

1. *Click the Account button at the bottom left as shown in the figure above.*

2. *This shows the user information for the Microsoft account.*

3. *This shows the details of any Microsoft connected services this user has.*

4. *This shows the version number of the Microsoft excel installed on your computer.*

5. *Checking the operating system*

6. *Click the "About Excel" button. A dialog window is displayed with information about your copy of Excel. See below.*

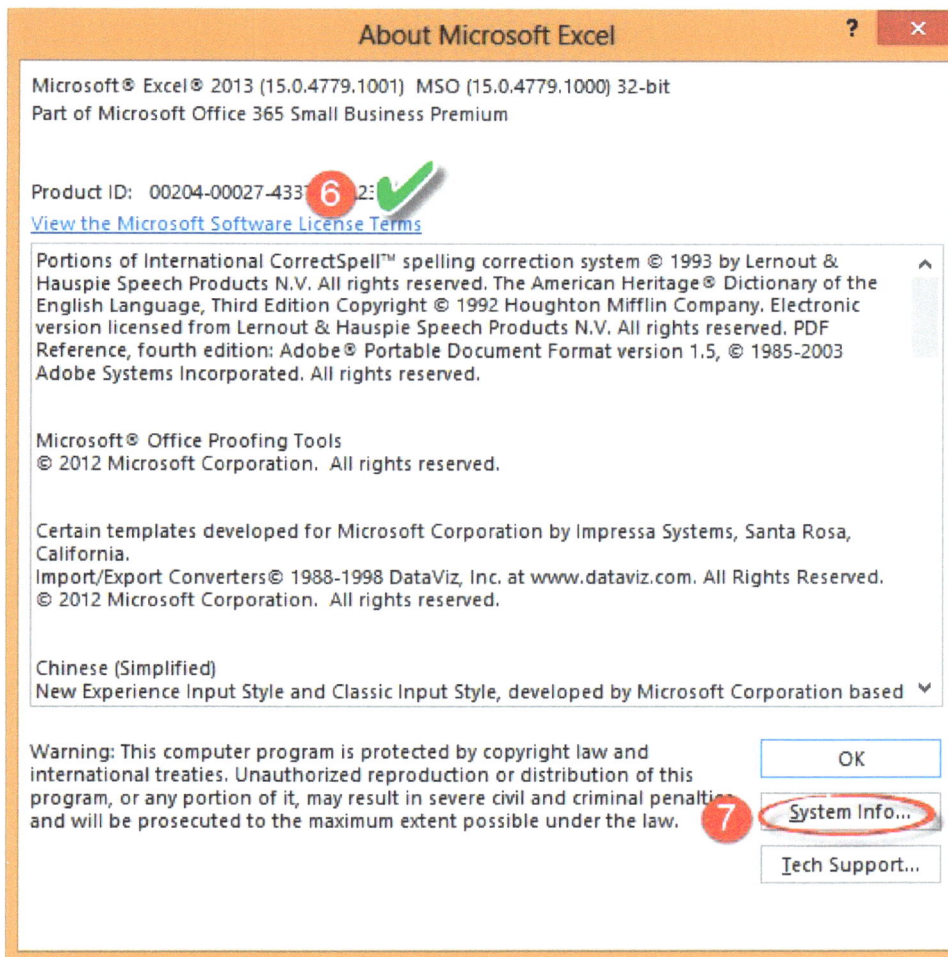

Fig. 4

1. *This is the product ID of your Microsoft excel that is installed on your computer.*

2. *Click the system info... button. The operating system (OS) Name and version will then be visible at the top right of the dialog window – See fig. 5.*

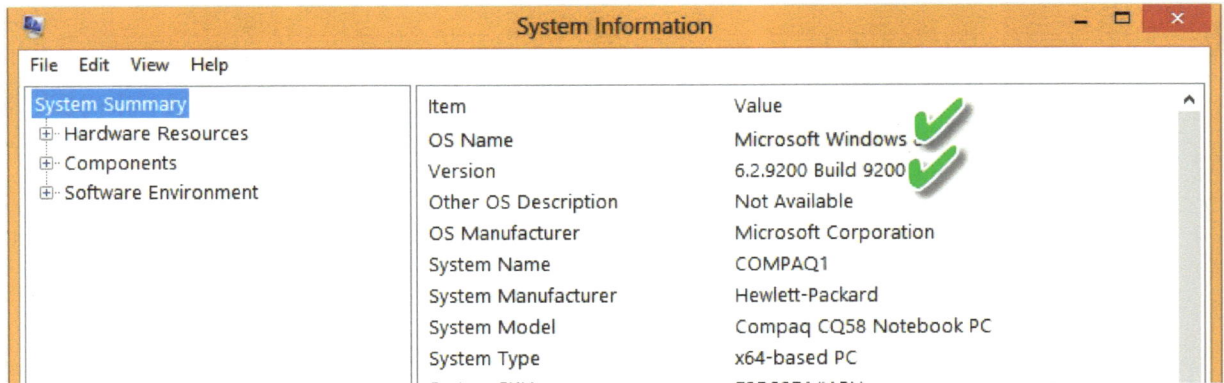

Fig. 5

- *Close the Excel window – see illustration below (click x at the top right hand corner)*

Fig.6

Pivot Tables

Let's begin, shall we?

You should have a sample data file for this exercise, if you don't, please download it from *www.sterlinglibs.com/files/pivot-table-data.xlsx*

1. *Open the pivot table data file. This worksheet contains a large table named Data. It contains 36 rows of transactional data (including headings) listing sales during the 12 month period from January 2015 to December 2015 inclusive.*

	Order No	Order Date	Client	Employee	Product	Category	Qty	Total
2	156438	02-Jan-15	Habadashes Academy	John,Fraser	phone message pads	Administrative supplies	14	122.76
3	156438	03-Jan-15	Habadashes Academy	John,Fraser	CD and disk rack or storage portfolio	Computer and Print Supplies	7	77.52
4	156438	04-Jan-15	Habadashes Academy	John,Fraser	wipe off board	Administrative supplies	25	250.60
5	156438	05-Jan-15	Habadashes Academy	John,Fraser	wall calendar for planning projects	Administrative supplies	14	107.72
6	156439	06-Jan-15	Kings Institute	Joyce,Antione	to-do list tracker	Administrative supplies	11	31.77
7	156440	07-Jan-15	Jumbo Electronic	Joyce,Antione	tape and glue	Desk Supplies	19	136.71
8	156440	08-Jan-15	Jumbo Electronic	Joyce,Antione	bulletin board with push pins	Administrative supplies	10	120.56
9	156440	09-Jan-15	Jumbo Electronic	Joyce,Antione	hanging file folders	Filing Supplies	9	88.74
10	156440	10-Jan-15	Jumbo Electronic	Mary,Stevenson	writable CD-Roms	Computer and Print Supplies	18	120.86
11	156441	11-Jan-15	Marks & Spenser	Mary,Stevenson	stapler, staple remover, and staples	Desk Supplies	6	12.19
12	156441	12-Jan-15	Marks & Spenser	Mary,Stevenson	compressed air cannister for cleaning	Computer and Print Supplies	4	30.06
13	156441	13-Jan-15	Marks & Spenser	Peter,Andrey	cable organizers	Computer and Print Supplies	16	163.74
14	156441	14-Jan-15	Marks & Spenser	Peter,Andrey	hole punch	Desk Supplies	1	7.79
15	156441	15-Jan-15	Marks & Spenser	Peter,Andrey	disk cleaning and repair kit	Computer and Print Supplies	8	63.79
16	156441	16-Jan-15	Marks & Spenser	Peter,Andrey	interior manila file folders	Filing Supplies	12	146.33
17	156442	17-Jan-15	Barclays Bank	Peter,Andrey	markers and highlighters	Desk Supplies	25	247.85
18	156442	18-Jan-15	Barclays Bank	Peter,Andrey	Rolodex or contact manager	Administrative supplies	10	37.77
19	156442	19-Jan-15	Barclays Bank	Martha,Tomlinson	scissors	Desk Supplies	9	43.16
20	156442	20-Jan-15	Barclays Bank	Martha,Tomlinson	back-up tape or Zip / Jaz disks	Computer and Print Supplies	6	55.76
21	156442	21-Jan-15	Barclays Bank	Martha,Tomlinson	ring binders	Filing Supplies	14	103.66
22	156442	22-Jan-15	Barclays Bank	Martha,Tomlinson	padded envelopes	Mailing Supplies	12	105.53

Fig. 7

If you want some suggested pivot tables, follow steps A-E below.

A. *Click anywhere inside the table.*

B. *Then, click insert at the top left side of the excel.*

C. *In the area under Tables, click "Recommended Pivot Tables". The recommended pivot tables window appears.*

5

D. *On the left hand side of the recommended pivot table's window, you can see a number of pivot tables. Whichever one you select a preview of it is displayed on the right hand side of the window.*

E. *Click the OK button to choose one of the recommended pivot tables if you so wish.*

See figure below.

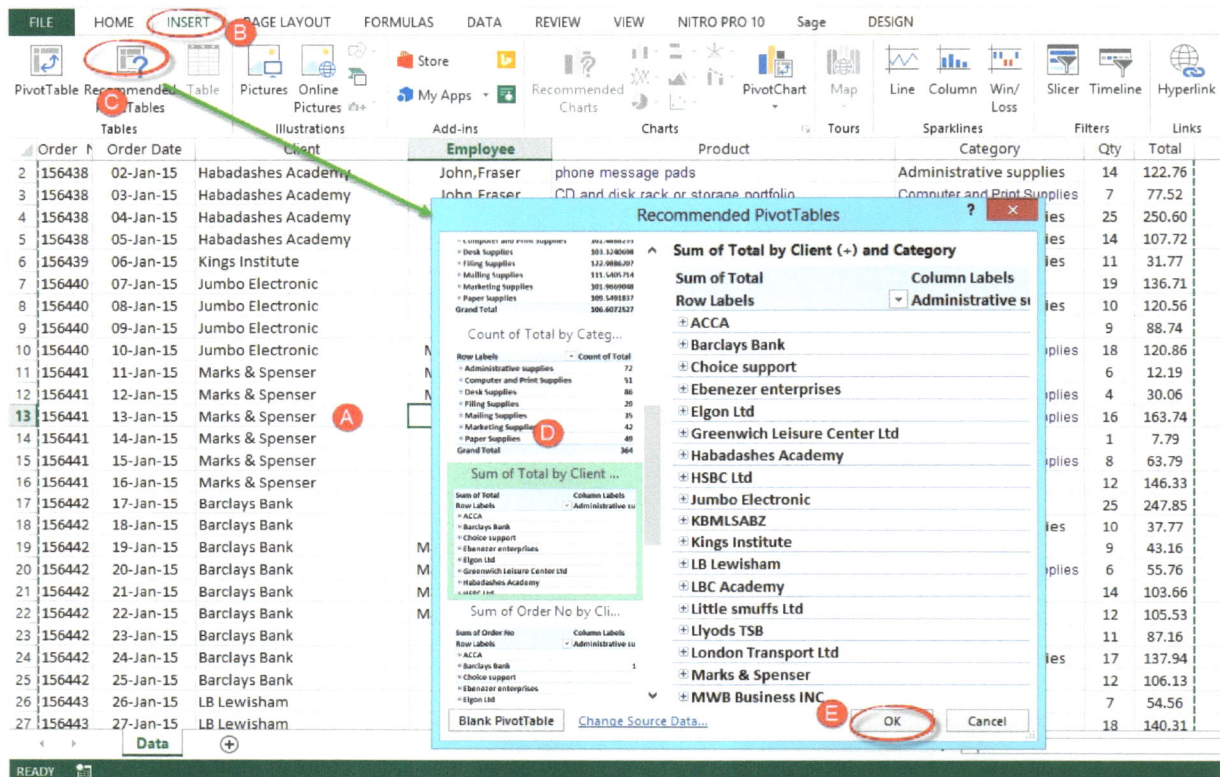

Fig. 8

I am sure if that was all it took to work with pivot tables, there would be no need for me writing this manual on pivot tables for you. Fair enough, there is a lot more to pivot tables than what excel can recommend for you like it did in the previous task.

Now, let's start this off a fresh, I would like for you to follow the instructions in the figure below; steps 1-6.

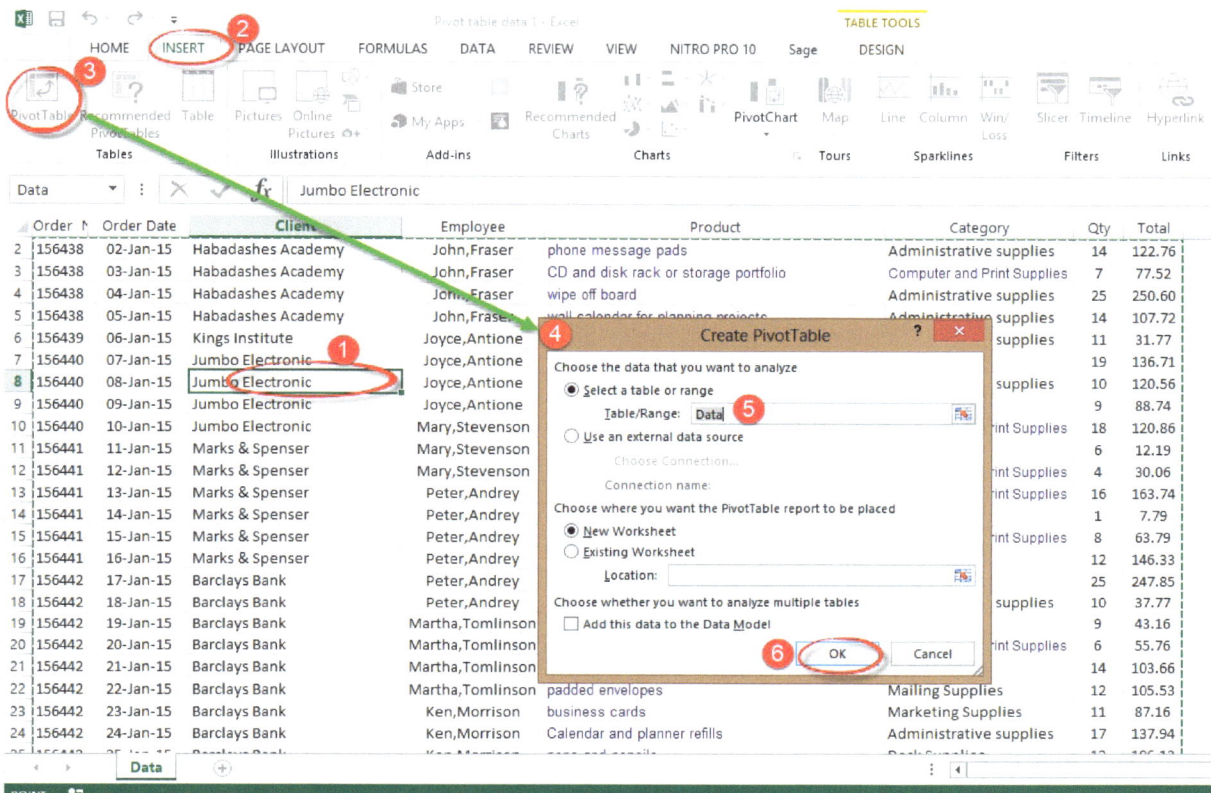

Fig. 9

1. *Click anywhere inside the table.*

2. *then; click insert at the top left side of the excel.*

3. *In the area under Tables click on Pivot Tables.*

4. *The first screen of the wizard appears.*

5. *Notice that, because you clicked inside the table, it has automatically detected the table's name of Data.*

6. *Click OK button.*

Notice that an empty pivot table is now shown on the screen (on the left side) and the Pivot Table Field List appears on the right of the screen – see fig. 10.

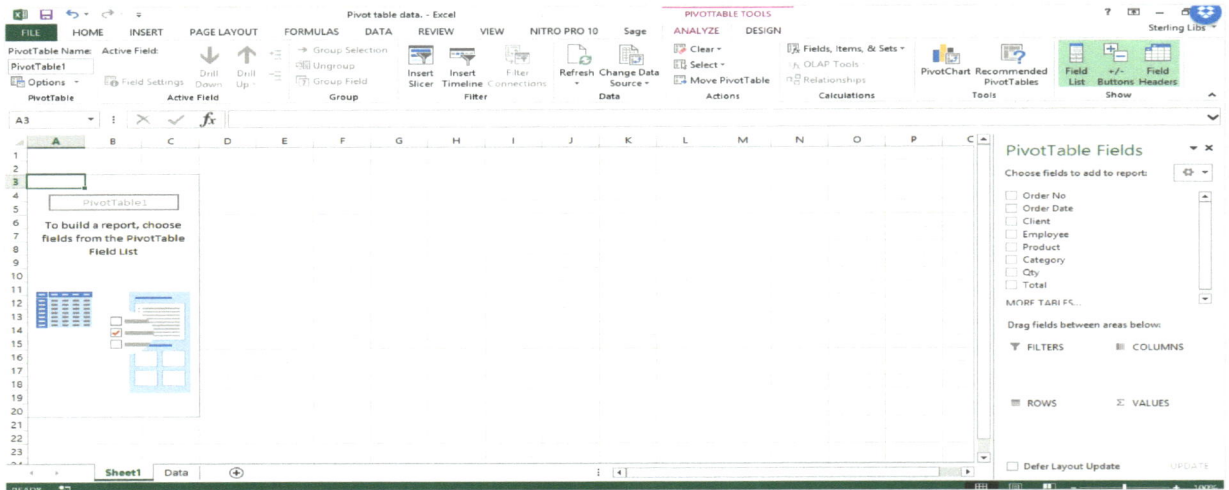

Fig. 10

Getting a sales report by category of items sold.

Check the Category, Qty and Total check boxes (in that order) on the Pivot Table Fields list, simply by clicking on three fields (steps 1, 2 & 3 as illustrated in the figure below).

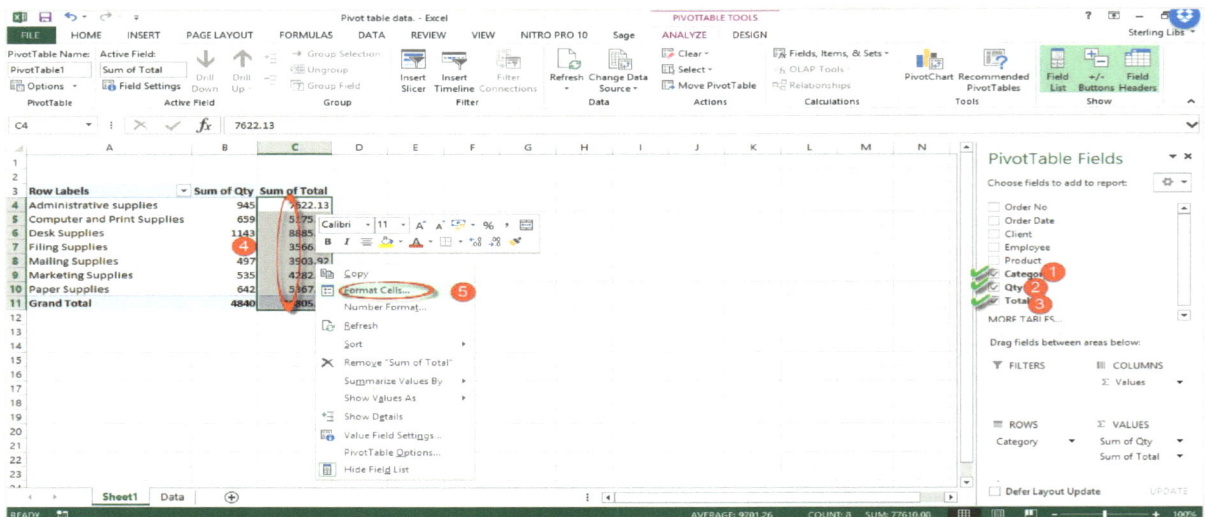

Fig. 11

Format the "Sum of Total" values shown in column C of the Pivot so that they show two decimal places as illustrated in fig. 12.

Select cell C4 – C11, then right click on the selection (step 4 as illustrated in the figure above)

Select Format cells from the window that appears (step 5 as illustrated in the figure above) and you will see a window similar to the one below:

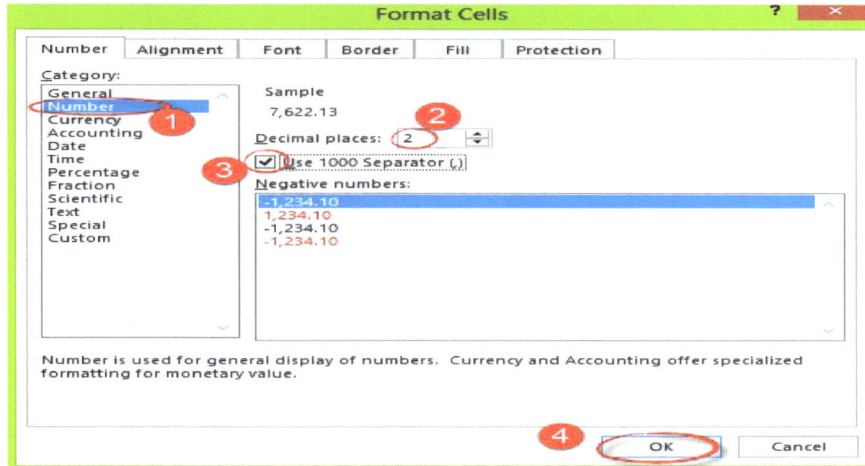

Fig. 12

Follow steps 1 – 4 as illustrated if the figure above and after step 4, your pivot table will look like the figure below. You have answered the question: What were my Sales by *Category!*

3	Row Labels	Sum of Qty	Sum of Total
4	Administrative supplies	945	7,622.13
5	Computer and Print Supplies	659	5,175.93
6	Desk Supplies	1143	8,885.87
7	Filing Supplies	419	3,566.67
8	Mailing Supplies	497	3,903.92
9	Marketing Supplies	535	4,282.61
10	Paper Supplies	642	5,367.91
11	Grand Total	4840	38,805.04

Fig. 13

Getting a sales report of units sold by each employee

Clear all check boxes on the PivotTable Fields list – (by unticking them) and then select the Employee and Qty check boxes. Yet again, with very little effort simply by doing this step, you have arrived at the answer to the answer to the question: How many units did each Employee sell? See fig. 14 & follow steps 1 – 2.

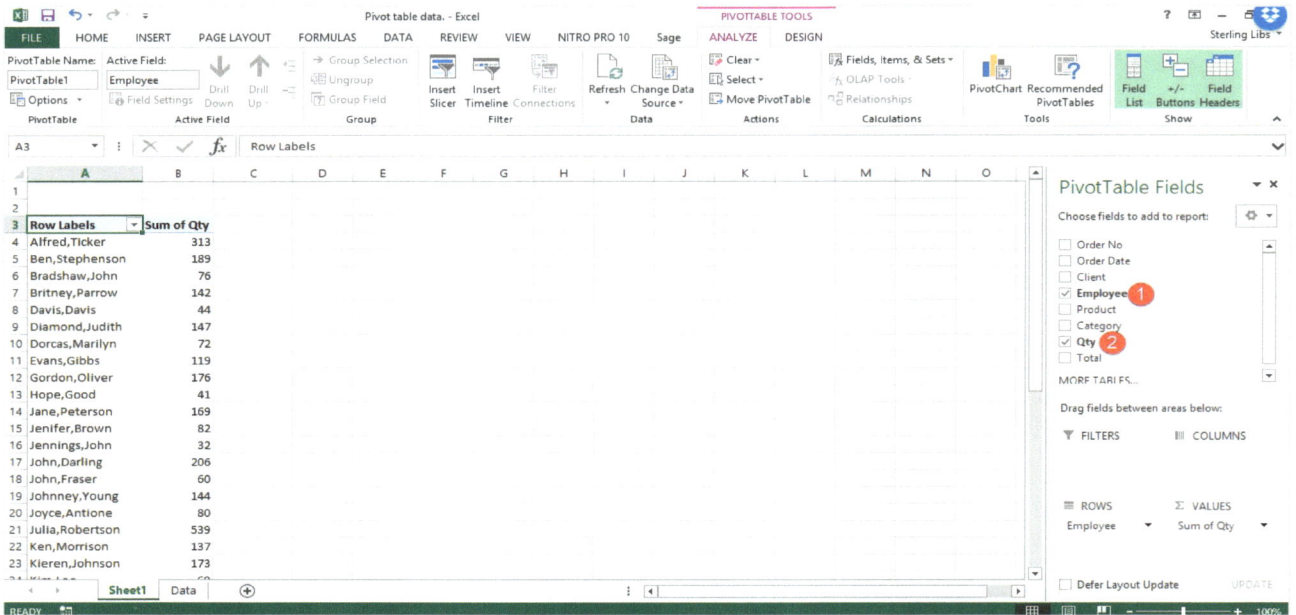

Fig. 14

Name the Pivot table Sales Data and name the pivot table work sheet; Pivot Table. Click "ANALYZE" under the "PIVOTTABLE TOOLS" then follow steps 1 & 2 as illustrated in the figure below

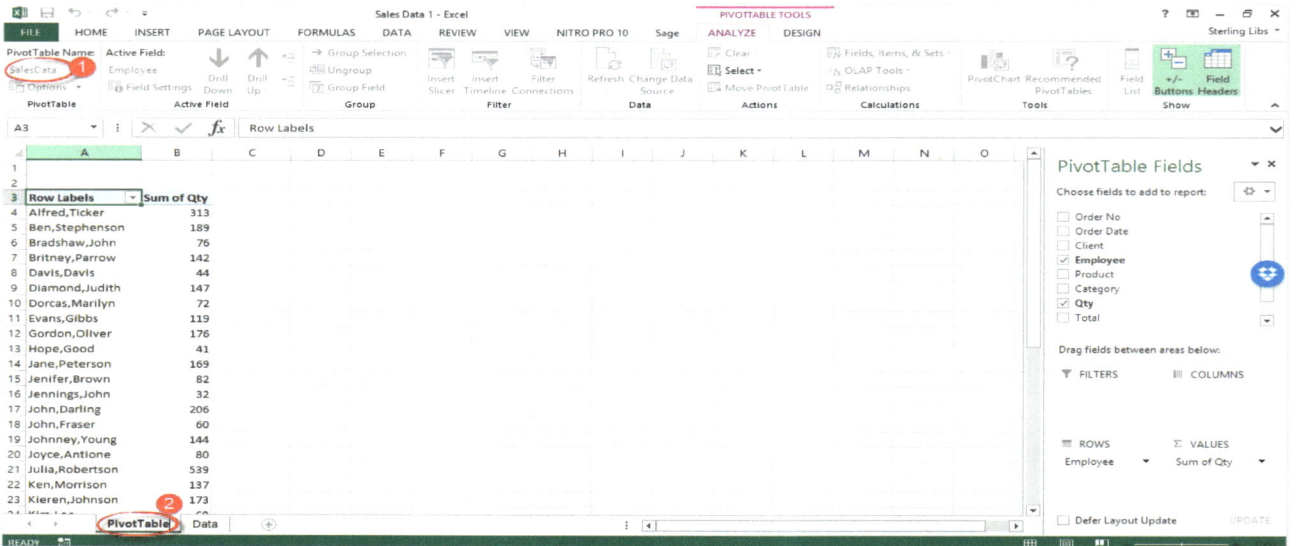

Fig. 15

Create a new folder (name it Pivot table) and save your work as Sales Data -1

How to create a grouped Pivot table report

From your new pivot table folder, open Sales Data -1 if it is not already open.

Select Pivot table worksheet then click inside the pivot table to show Pivot table field list.

1. *Click Category on the pivot table list. Each employee's sales for each Category are now shown in the report.*

2. *Click Product to add a Product information to the pivot table. The report now breaks the sales down by Employee, Category and Product.*

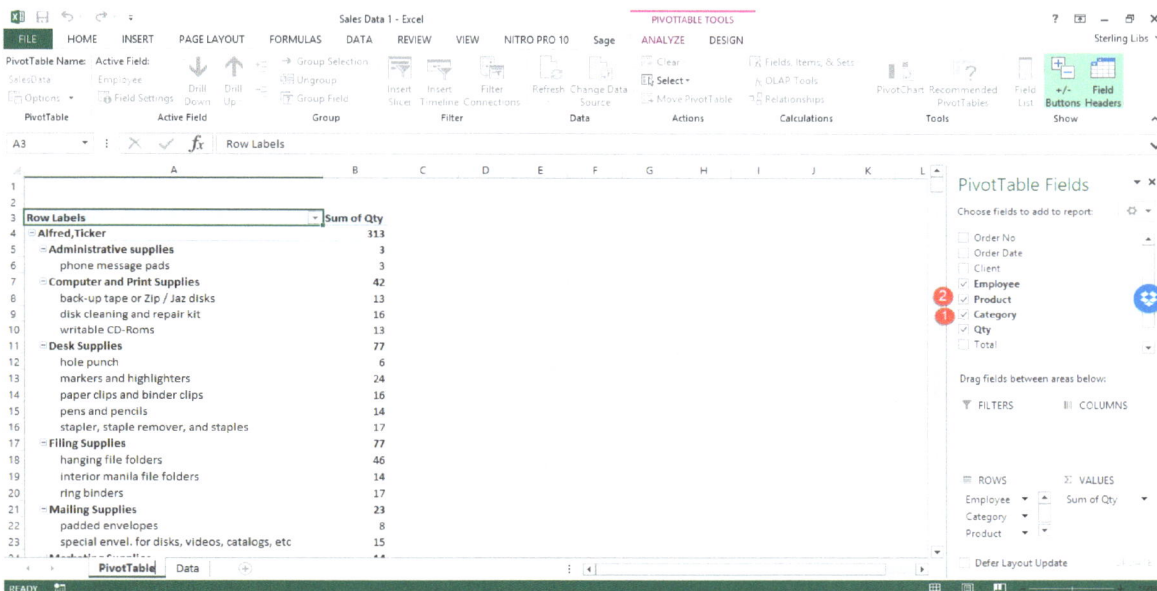

Fig. 16

3. *Collapse the outline to show only sales by Employee: Right click cell A4, a shortcut menu appears. Click Expand/Collapse > Collapse Entire Field. The pivot table collapses to level of Employee. See steps 1 – 3 in fig. 17.*

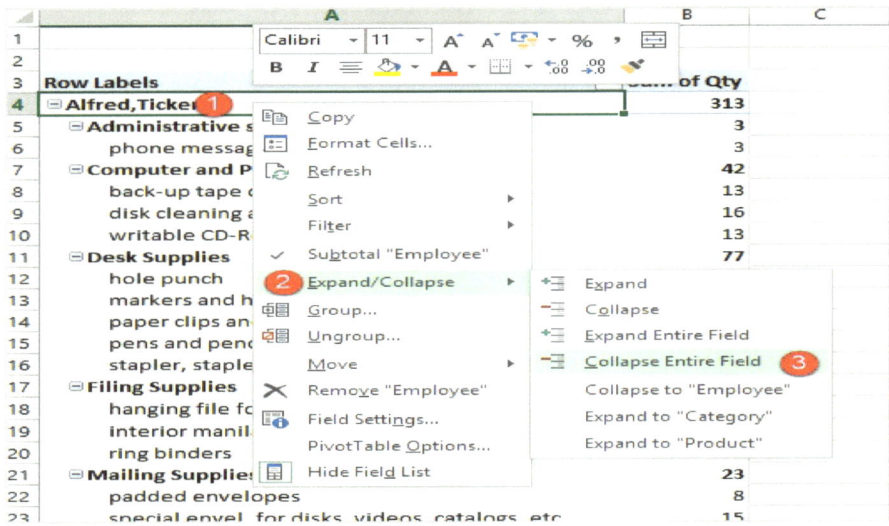

Fig. 17

After step 3 as illustrated in the figure above, the pivot table will look as figure below.

Row Labels	Sum of Qty
Alfred,Ticker	313
Ben,Stephenson	189
Bradshaw,John	76
Britney,Parrow	142
Davis,Davis	44
Diamond,Judith	147
Dorcas,Marilyn	72
Evans,Gibbs	119
Gordon,Oliver	176
Hope,Good	41

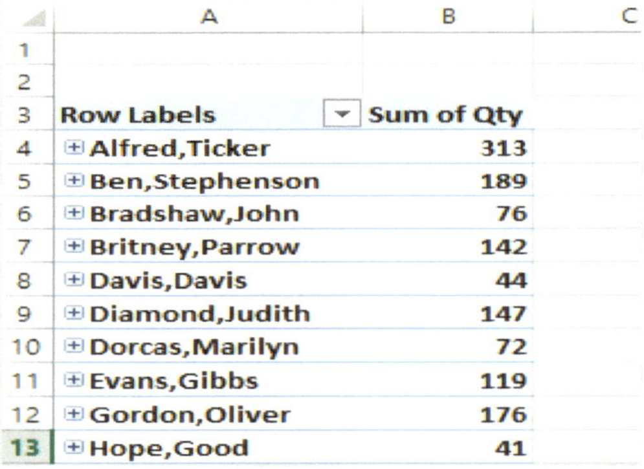

Fig. 18

Expand John Bradshaw's sales to show full details. Click the small + sign to the left of cell A6

Collapse the outline by clicking on the small – sign on cell A6 so that Bradshaw's sales by Category are shown without Product details.

Save your work as Sales Data-2

Understanding Pivot Table rows and columns

Open your saved Sales Data -2 if it is not already open.

Select the pivot table worksheet and click inside the pivot table to display the Pivot Table Field List. At the moment, we have three columns in the Row Labels list and one in Values list. This creates a pivot table that shows sales first by Employee, then grouped by Category and then grouped by Product.

1.   *Remove the Category and Product rows from the Row labels field by clicking first the Category and when the shortcut menu appears, click on Remove Field. Do the same with the Product menu.*

2.   *Add the Category to the pivot table Column label. Drag it from the Pivot Table List Field List to the Column Labels list. The pivot table now shows sales for each employee by Category with the Category's listed along the top row as column labels.*

3.   *Add the Product field to the Column Labels list in just the same way as you did the category in step 2 above. PivotTable now looks like the figure below.*

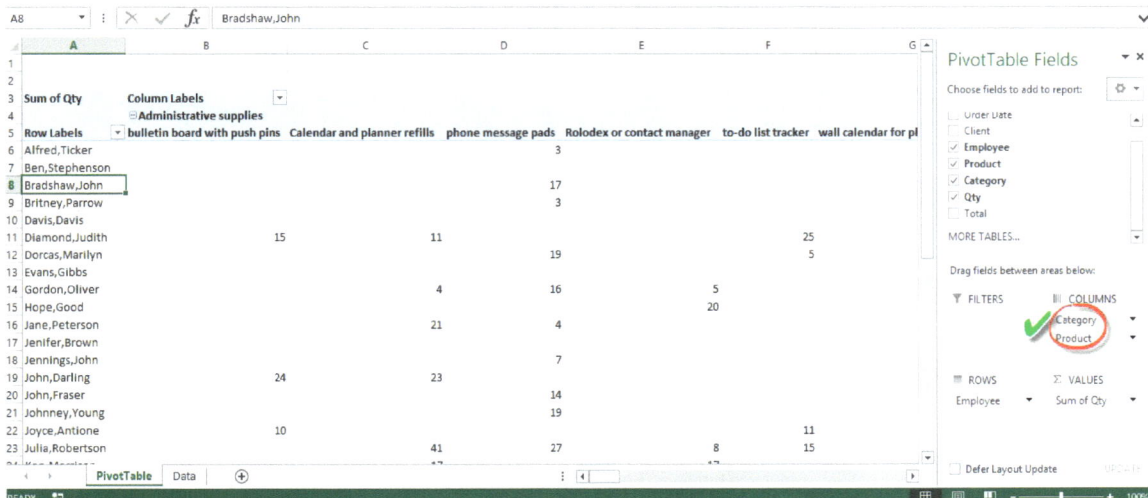

Fig. 19

4.   *Save your work as Sales Data-3*

Apply a simple filter and sort to a pivot table

Open Sales Data-3 if it not already open and select pivot table worksheet and click inside it.

1. *Remove the Category and Product Column labels.*

2. *Click drop-down arrow next to Row Labels in cell A3 (Step A as illustrated in the figure below) and filter the pivot table so that only female employees are shown (Step B – untick all the names that seem male and only leave female names ticked) – see figure below.*

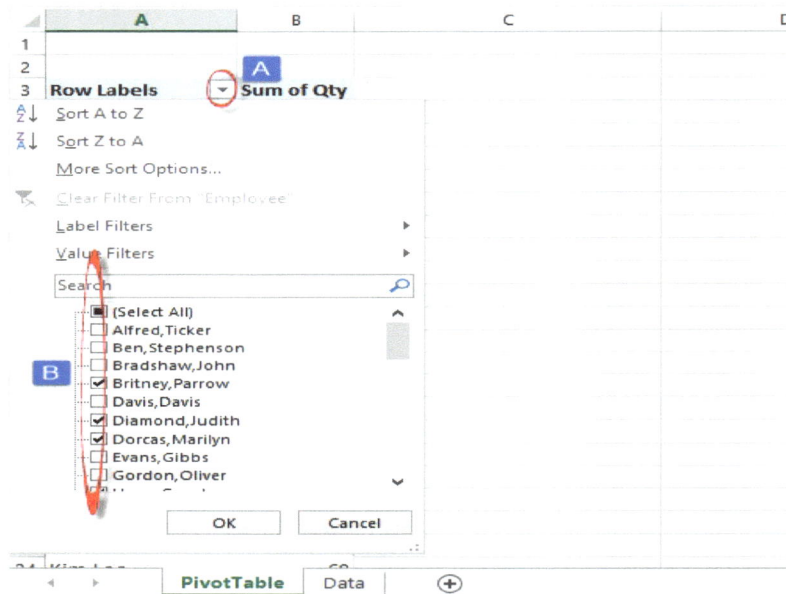

Fig. 20

3. *Sort the employee names in Z-A order by following steps A & B in fig. 21.*

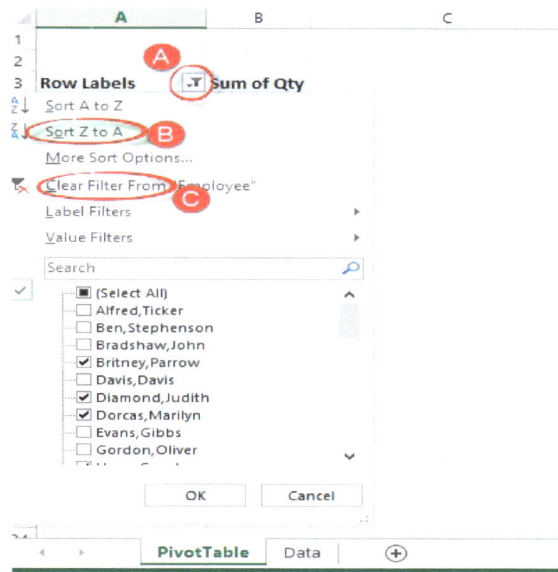

Fig. 21

4. *Remove the filter - Step C in figure above and save your work as Sales Data-4*

Using the report filter field

Open Sales data-4 if it is not already open and then select pivot table worksheet and click on it

1. *Drag the Category field from PivotTable Fields list to the Report Filters list. Notice that a filter has appeared at the top left of the pivot table (in cells A1 & B1). The report filter currently shows all Categories. You can use the report filter to display sales of any Category by clicking the drop-down list arrow in Cell B1 and clicking any Category*

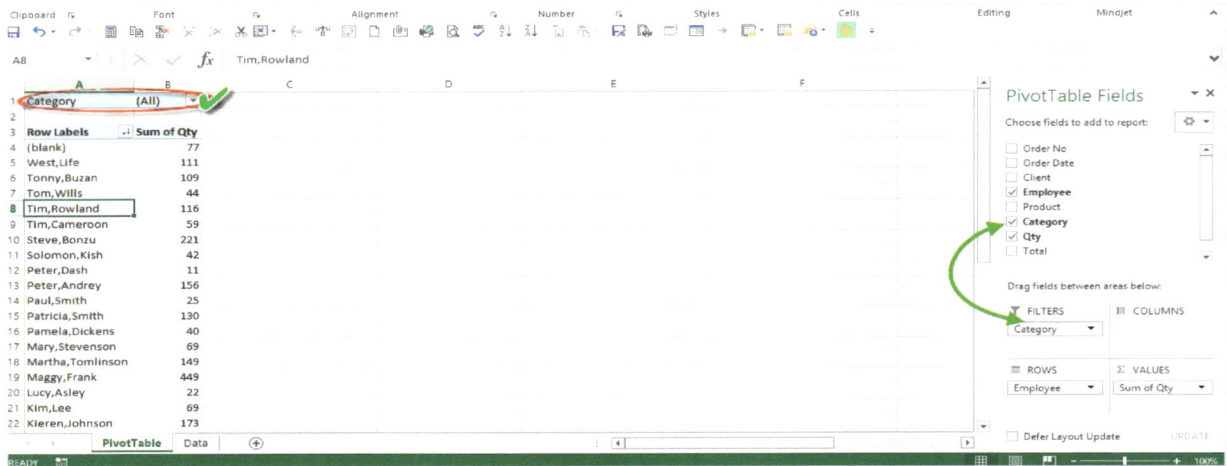

Fig. 22

2. For example, use the report filter field to show sales in Desk Supplies category for May & June 2015. To do this, first drag the Order date field from the PivotTable Field List down to the Report Filter List. Now select the Desk Supplies category by clicking on the drop-down list for Category in cell B1 and selecting Desk Supplies.

Here is how your work looks like now.

Fig. 23

3. Now, click the drop-down arrow in cell B2.

4. Make sure that the Select Multiple Items check box is checked.

5. *Uncheck the (All) check box*

6. *Scroll down the list and check all of the May & June 2015 check boxes.*

7. *Click OK. Only goods sold in the Desk Supplies Category during May & June 2015 are now displayed.*

See figure below for an illustration (A-E) of how to do steps 3-7 above.

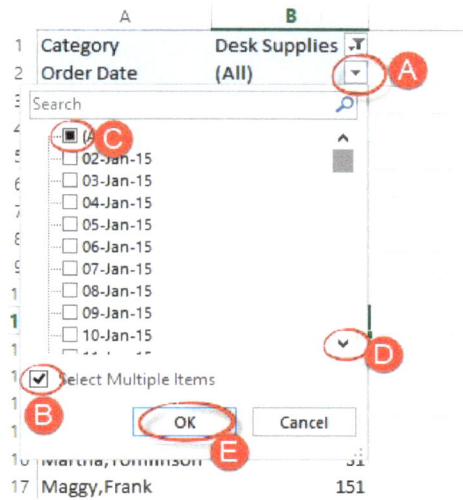

Fig. 24

Here is how your work should look like so far after step E in the illustration shown in the figure above.

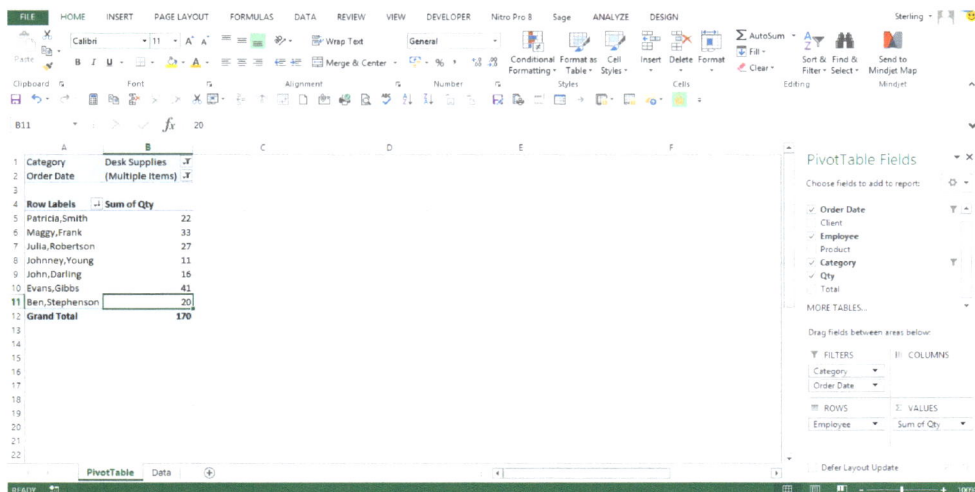

Fig. 25

8. *Save your work as Sales Data -5.*

Creating multiple pages automatically by using report filter fields

Here, we cater for the following scenario:

You have been asked to print out a sales listing for each employee. This involves printing a total of 24 separate reports. It is easy, but time consuming, to print each sheet manually. You would need to perform 24 filter and print operations. Could there be a better way?

Surely there is! We can use a report filter to automate the whole task and print all 24 reports in one operation.

Open Sales Data -5, select PivotTable worksheet and remove all filters.

1. *Change the fields displayed by the pivot table as follows:*

   a. *Under the Repot filter list, drag the Employee field.*

   b. *Under the Row labels list, drag the Category field.*

   c. *Under the Values field list, drag the Qty total field.*

Notice that the Values field automatically appears in the Column Labels list when you add more than one field to the Values List.

Fig. 26

2. *Now, create separate worksheets detailing each employee's sales:*

   a. *Click anywhere within the pivot table. Then click PivotTable Tools > Analyze> Options > Show Report Filter Pages. The Show Report Filter Pages dialog window appears, and because there is only one report filter, there's only one choice (Employee). If you had multiple report filters, you could choose which filter you wanted to use.*

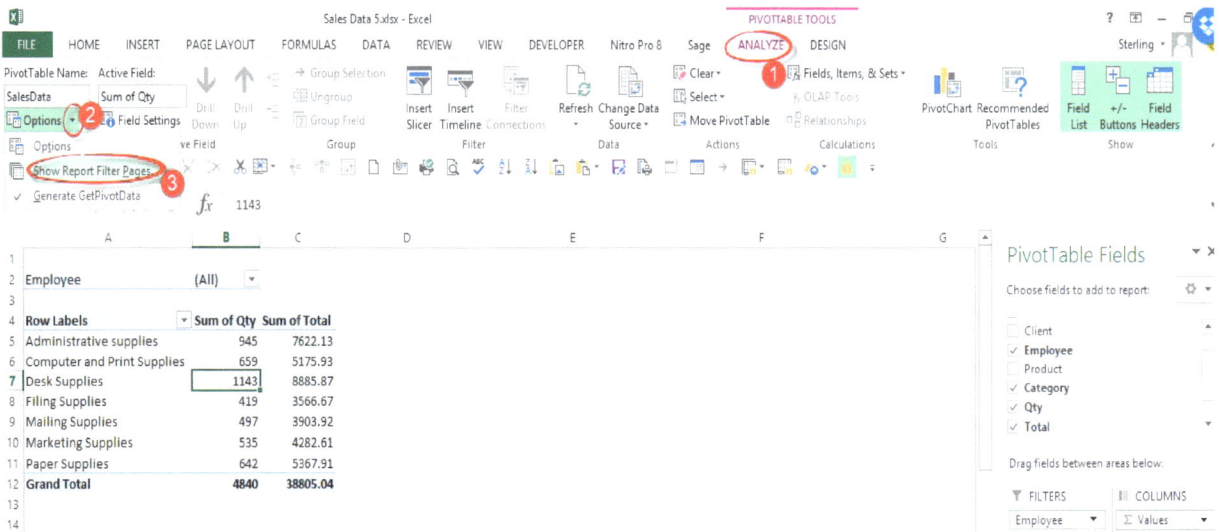

Fig. 27

After step 3 as illustrated in the figure above, a window similar to the one below will appear.

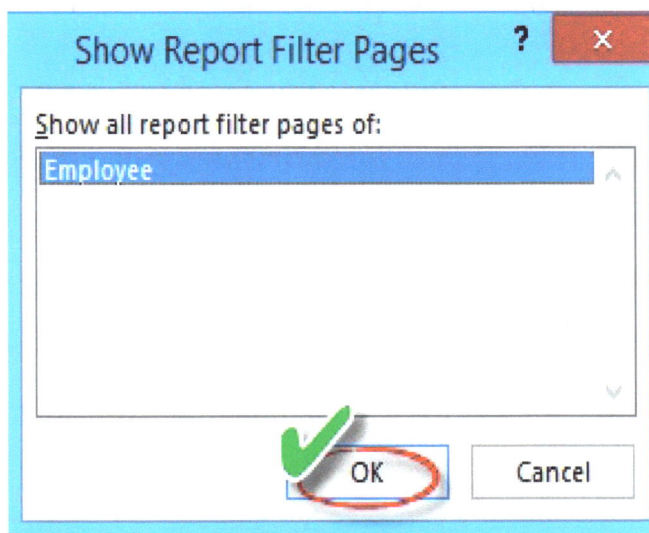

Fig. 28

b.   Click OK, and Immediately you click OK, all the worksheets corresponding to each employee are instantly created, one for each employee.

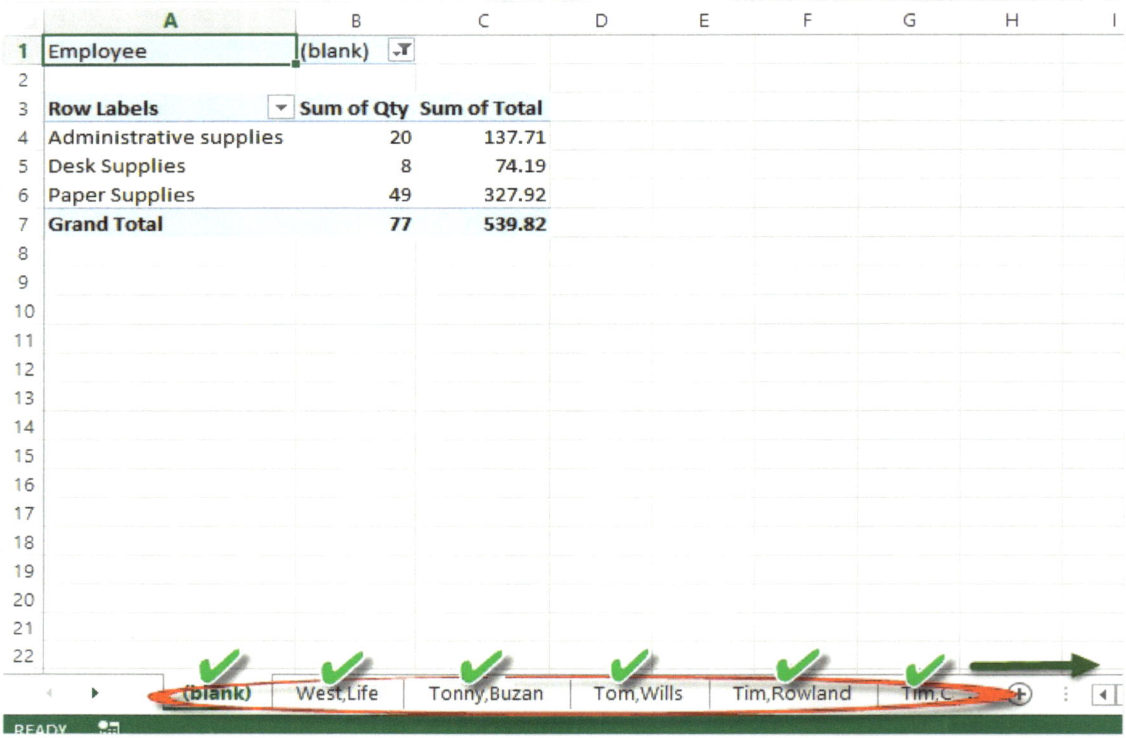

Fig. 29

3.   Print/preview all the worksheet**s.**

   a.   Click on the first employee (Blank)

   b.   Hold down the <**Shift**> Key

   c.   Use the worksheet scroll bar buttons so that the last employee's tab is visible

   d.   Click on the last employee's tab (Alfred, Ticker). You have now selected all of the employee worksheets.

   e.   Click: FILE button at the top left corner of the Excel then select "Print". Note that the Active Sheets is selected by default and you can see the preview of the 1 of the 38 employee reports.

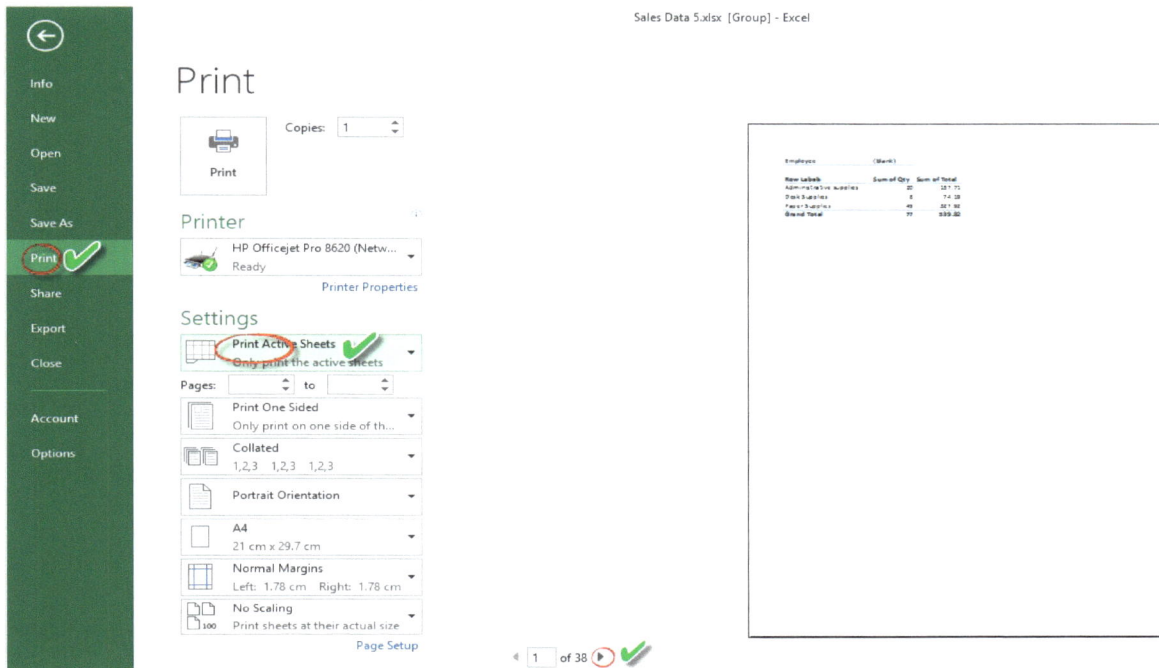

Fig. 30

4. *Close the preview button.*

5. *Save your work as multiple sheets -1.*

Pivot Table styles

Format a pivot table using PivotTable styles

Open Sales Data -5 from your pivot table folder.

1. *Romove all existing fields from the pivot table. You can do this faster by dragging each field from the field selection panes to the field list above.*

2. *Show the following: On the Row labels, show Employee, on the Column Label, show Category and on the Values, show Sum of Total.*

Here is how it looks after those two steps - see fig. 31.

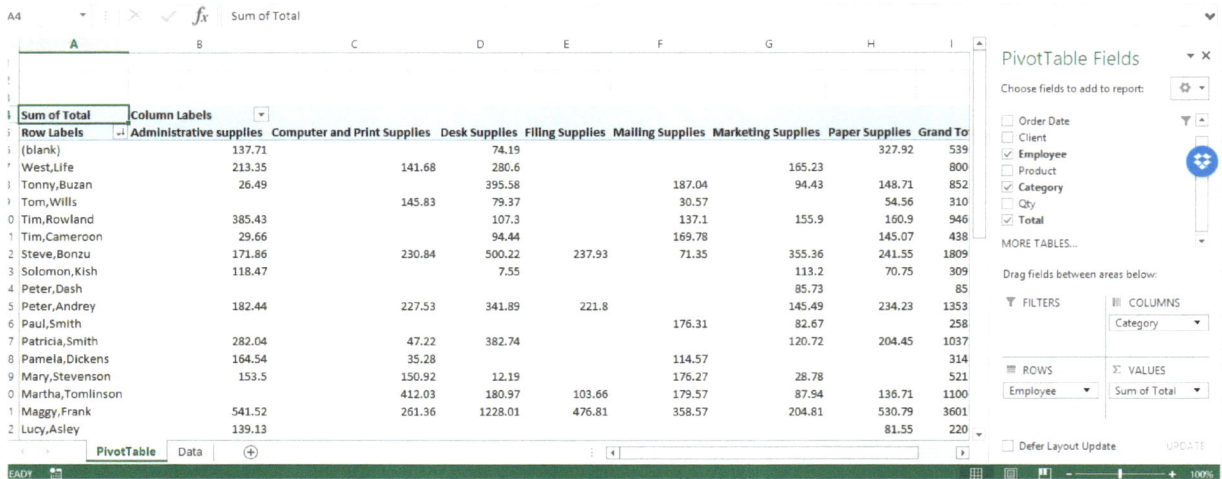

Fig. 31

3. *Filter to only show the Administrative, Computer & Print and Desk Supplies (9 Step A in the figure below) and also filter to show only the following employees: Peter Andrey, Patricia Smith and Pamela Dickens (Step B in the figure below).*

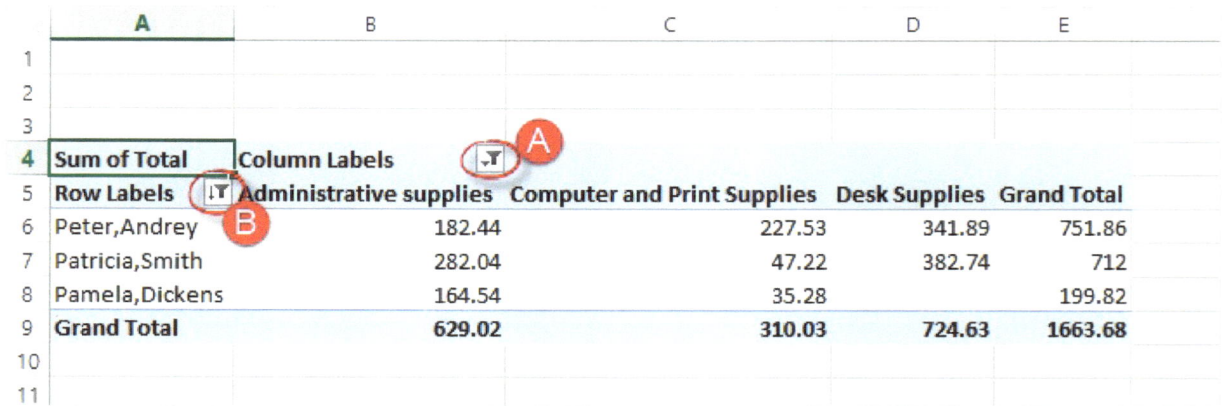

Fig. 32

4. *Apply the PivotTable Style: Dark 9. Do this by Clicking PivotTable Tools > Design >Pivot Table Styles > Dark >Pivot style Dark 9. (Follow steps A-D in fig. 33).*

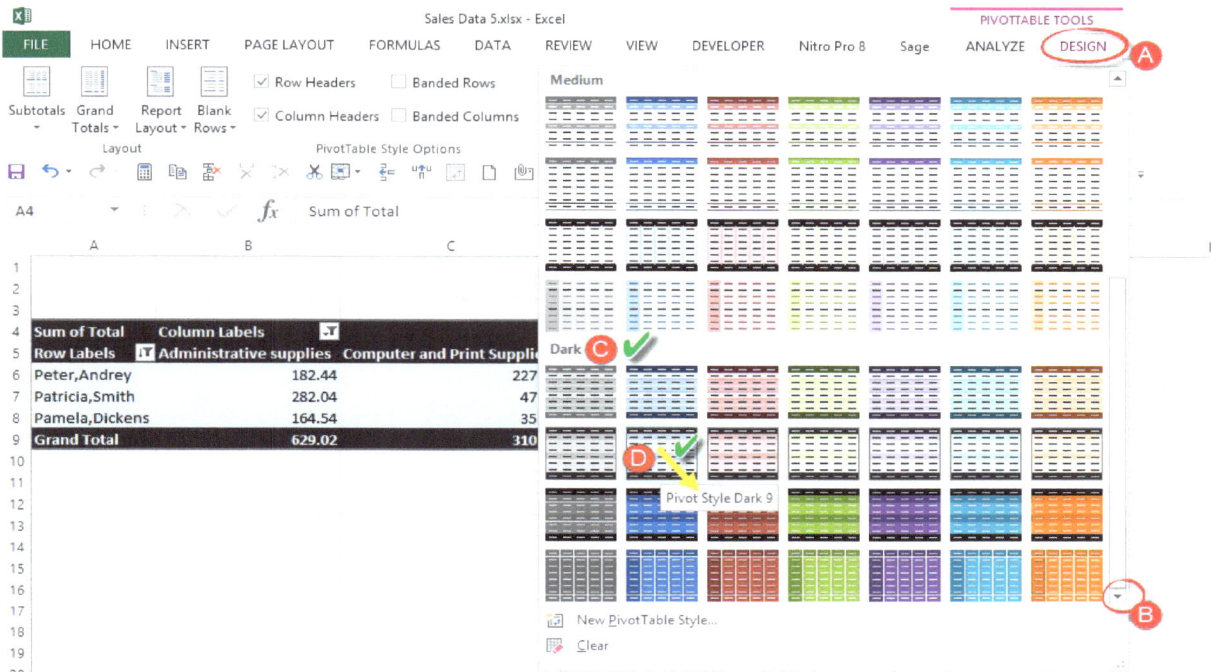

Fig. 33

5. *Enable banded Rows and Banded Columns by: Click PivotTable Tools > Design >Pivot Table Style Options > Tick Banded Rows check box & > Tick Banded Columns check box. See figure below.*

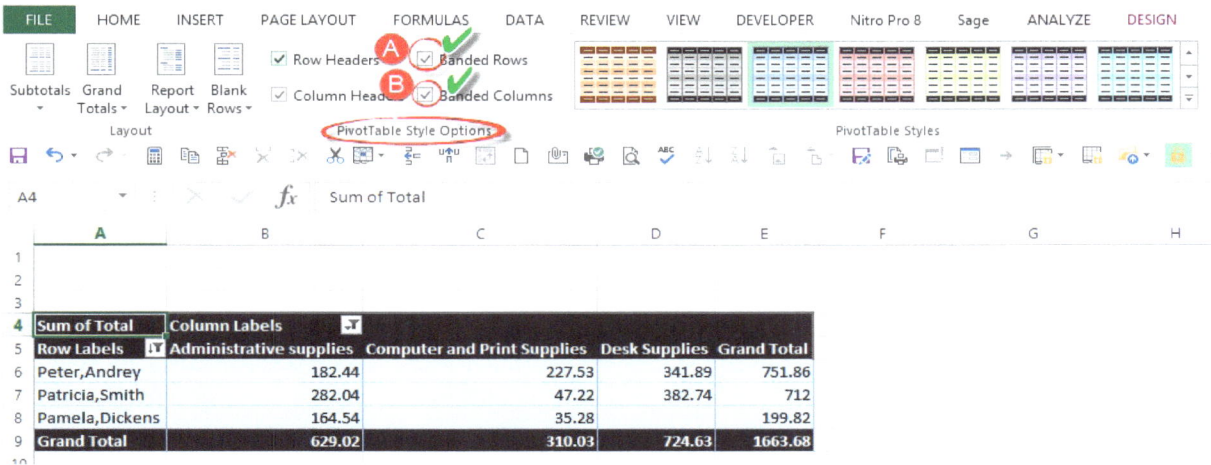

Fig. 34

6. *Save your work as Sales Data -6.*

Creating a custom Pivot Table Style

Open Sales Data -6 from your sample files folder (if it is not already open) and remove the existing style by first clicking on the pivot table to activate it, then click on PivotTable Tools > Design > PivotTable Styles > Light > None.

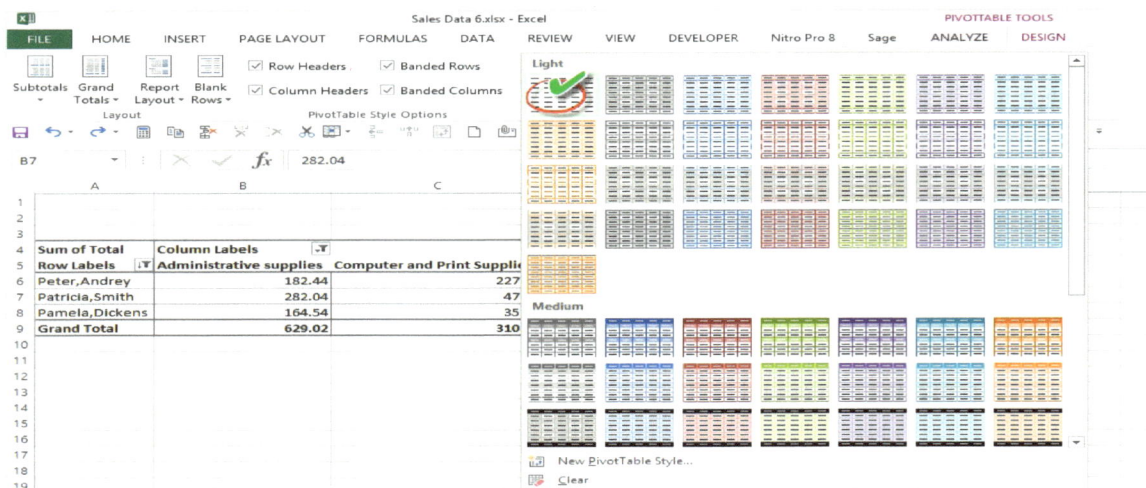

Fig. 35

Create a custom pivot table style called Excellence by duplicating the *Medium8* built in style

a. *Select PivotTable Style Medium 8 from the PivotTable design tab. Right click on it and click on Duplicate from the shortcut menu that appears (as shown in the figure below). The Modify PivotTable Quick Style dialog window appears (see fig. 37).*

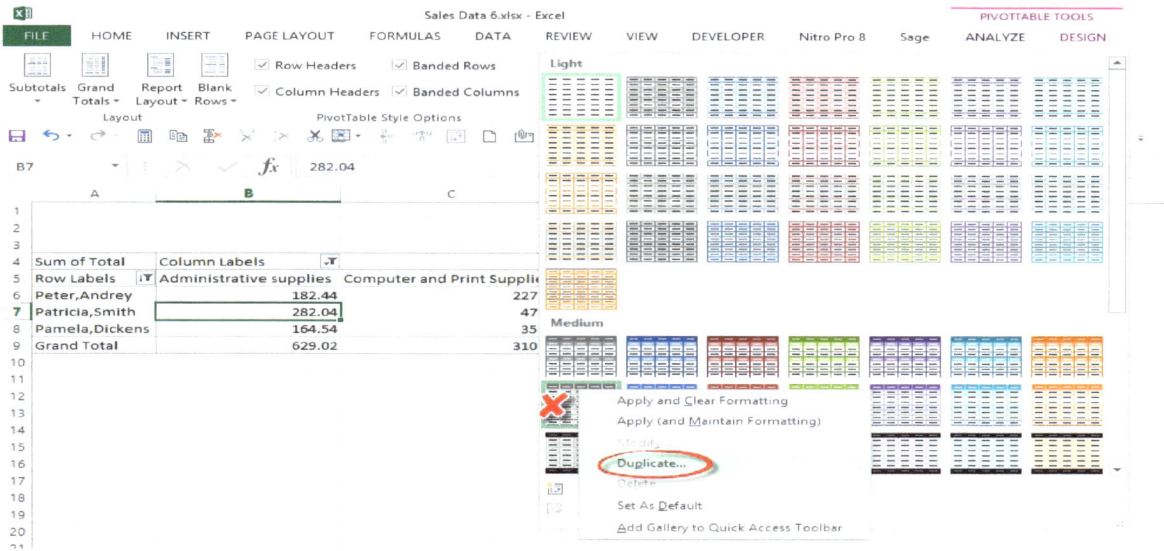

Fig. 36

b.   *Type the name* **Excellence** *into the Name Text box and click OK.*

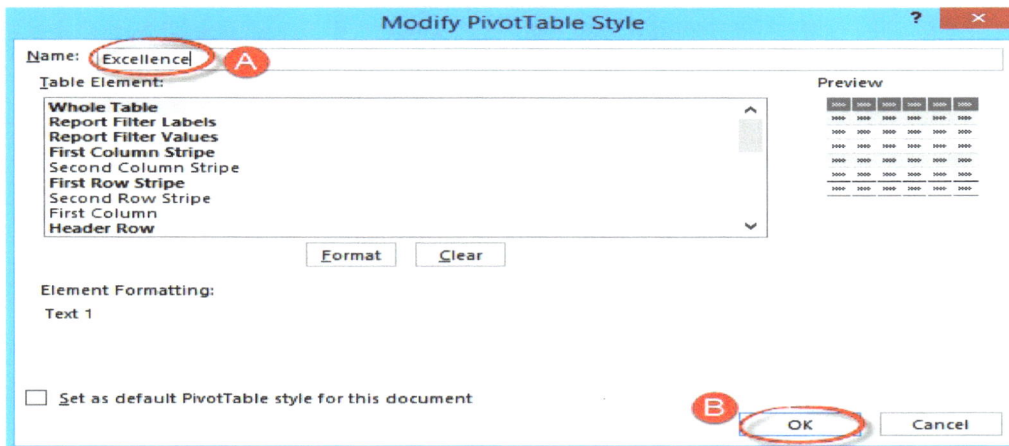

Fig. 37

c.   *Now Apply the new Excellence style to the pivot table by clicking on the design tab of the pivot table tools and selecting Excellence.*

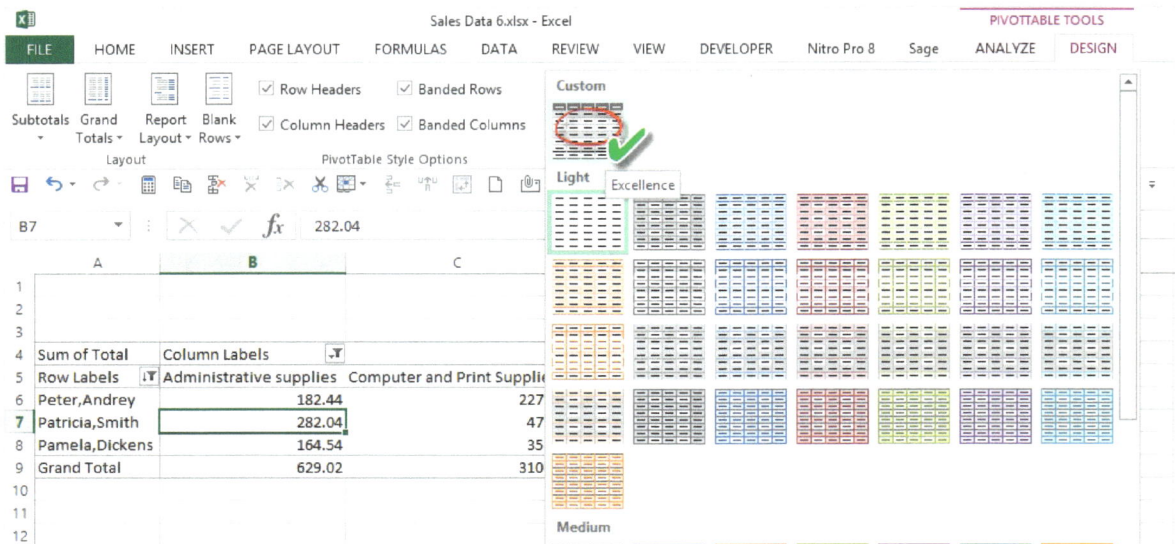

Fig. 38

Modify the Excellence Style so that it shows the Grand Totals column in bold face.

a. *Select the Excellence style through the pivot table design tab.*

b. *Right click on it and select* **Modify** *from the short cut menu that appears*

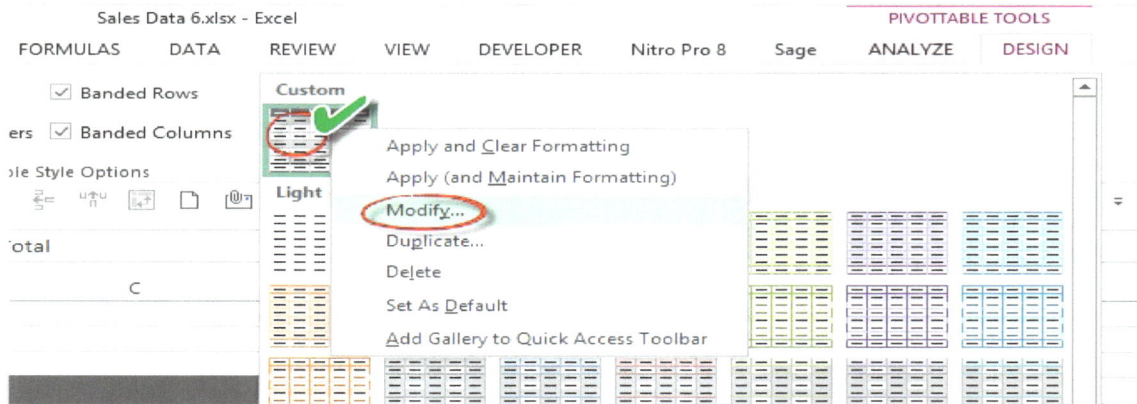

Fig. 39

a. *Click the down arrow to scroll down – see fig. 40.*

b. *Select* **Grand Total Column** *from the table element list.*

c. *Click format button and select the font tab.*

d. *Select the font style: Bold.*

e. *Click OK, then*

f. *OK again. The grand total column is now shown in bold.*

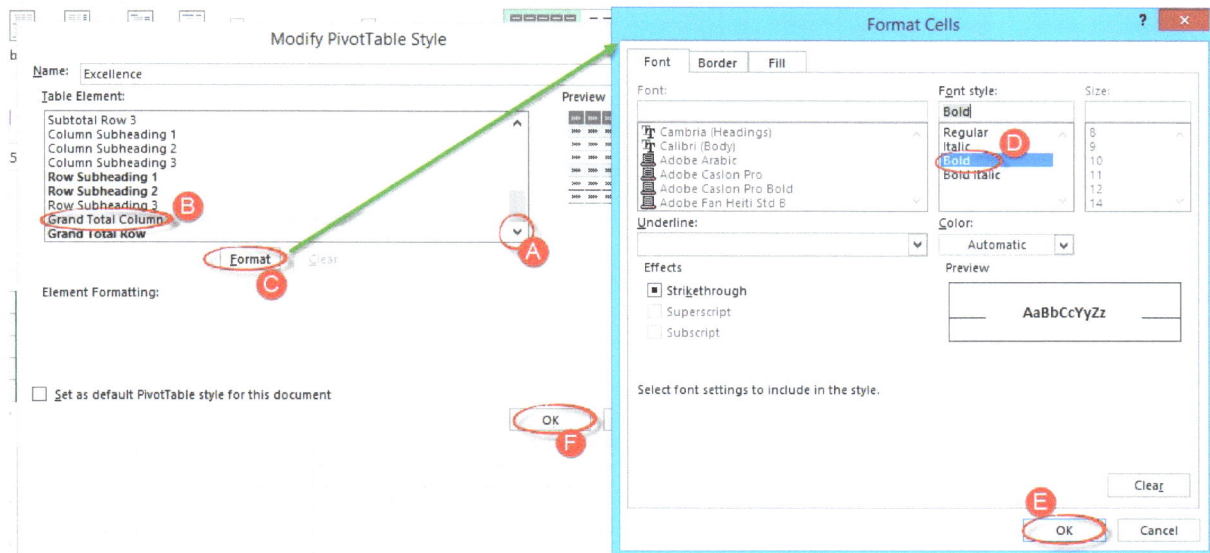

Fig. 40

Save your work as Sales Data -7.

Pivot Table Report Layouts

1. *Open Sales Data -7 from your pivot table folder and remove all existing fields from the pivot table by dragging them up into the PivotTable Fields List.*

2. *Put the Employee field into Row Labels, followed by the Category Field. After that, Put the total field into the Values field.*

3. *Expand the Employee field in the pivot table (Click on the + sign in cell A5, A6, A7) to also show the categories.*

4. *Change the report layout to Tabular form through the design tab of the Pivot table tools and by selecting the report layout from the layout section. See fig. 41.*

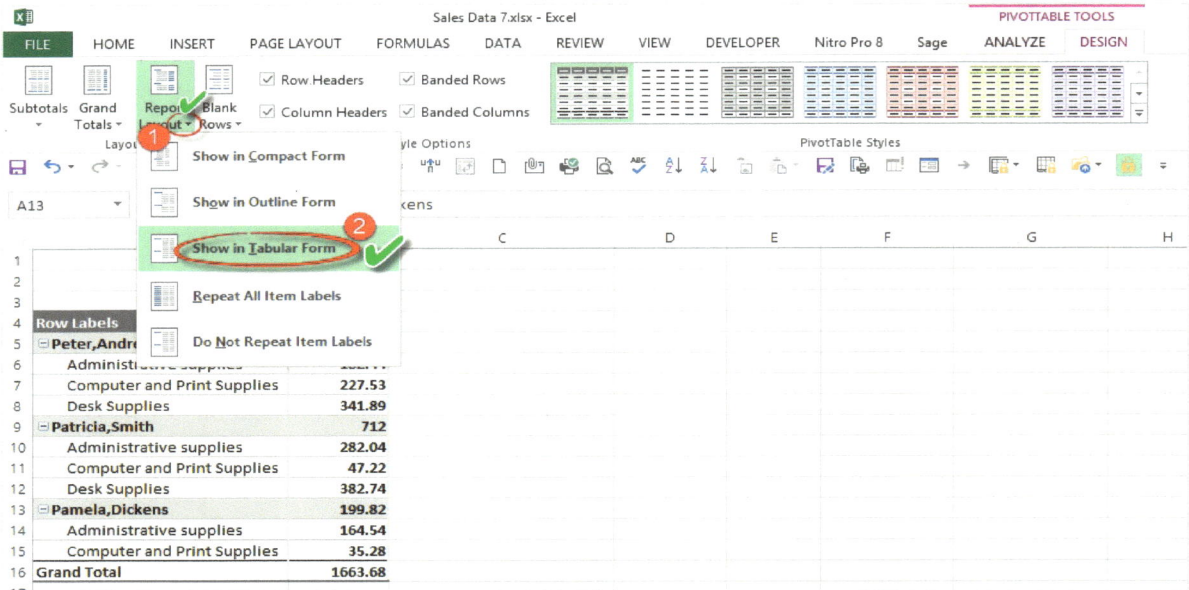

Fig. 41

After step 2 as illustrated in the figure above, your Pivot table will look like the figure below.

Employee	Category	Sum of Total
⊟ Peter,Andrey	Administrative supplies	182.44
	Computer and Print Supplies	227.53
	Desk Supplies	341.89
Peter,Andrey Total		751.86
⊟ Patricia,Smith	Administrative supplies	282.04
	Computer and Print Supplies	47.22
	Desk Supplies	382.74
Patricia,Smith Total		712
⊟ Pamela,Dickens	Administrative supplies	164.54
	Computer and Print Supplies	35.28
Pamela,Dickens Total		199.82
Grand Total		1663.68

Fig. 42

5. *Save your work as Sales Data -8.*

How to add/remove subtotals and apply formatting to pivot table fields

Open Sales Data -8 and apply a filter to show only the Administrative, Computer and Print, and Desk supplies.

1. *Add the Product field to the Row label.*

2. *Hover the mouse cursor over the left edge of the Administrative supplies Total in Cell B9. Make sure you see the black arrow cursor shape and then click to select. Notice that when you select the field, all the category subtotal cells are selected.*

3. *Click: Home > Styles > Cell Styles > Total (as shown in the figure below). The Total style is applied to all Category subtotal fields.*

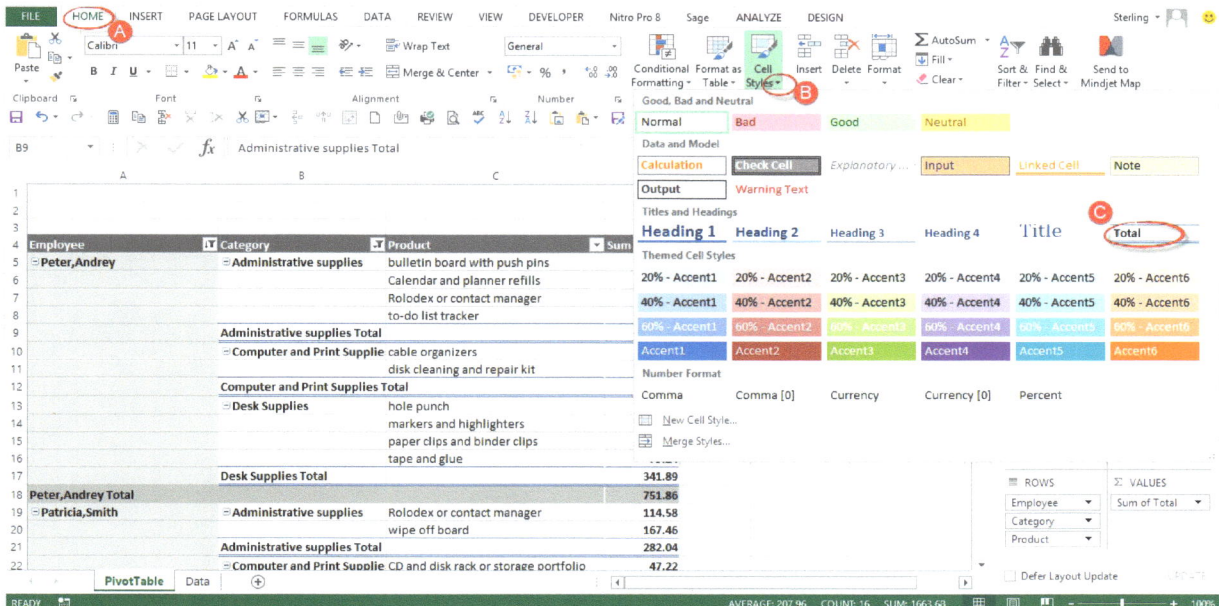

Fig. 43

After step C as illustrated in the figure above, here is how your pivot table now looks like - fig. 44.

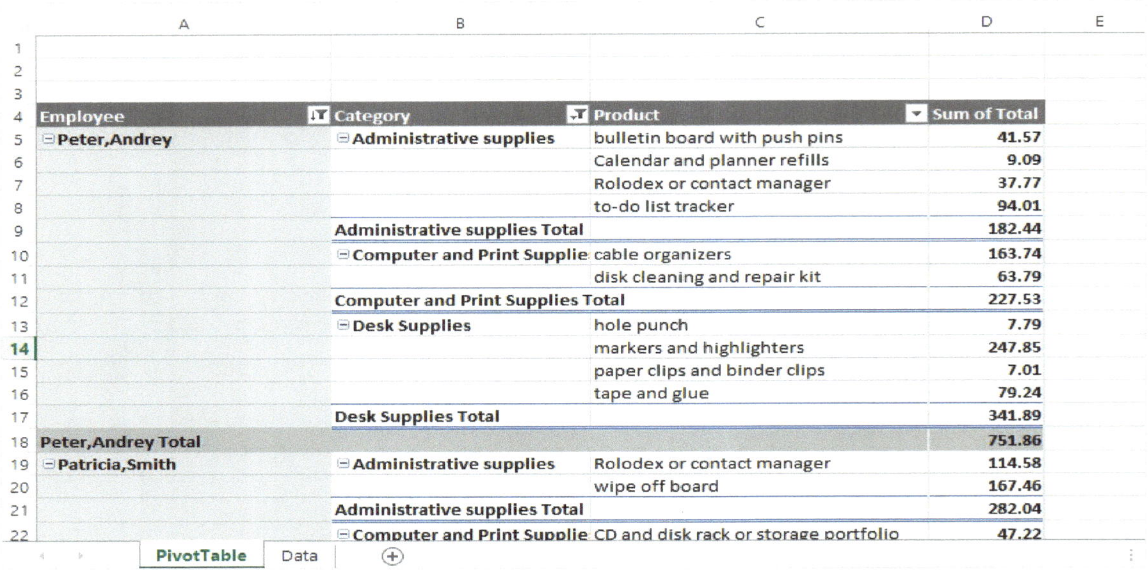

Fig. 44

4. *Remove Category subtotals by right clicking on any category in column B then clicking Subtotal "Category" on the shortcut menu that appears. The Category subtotal fields is removed.*

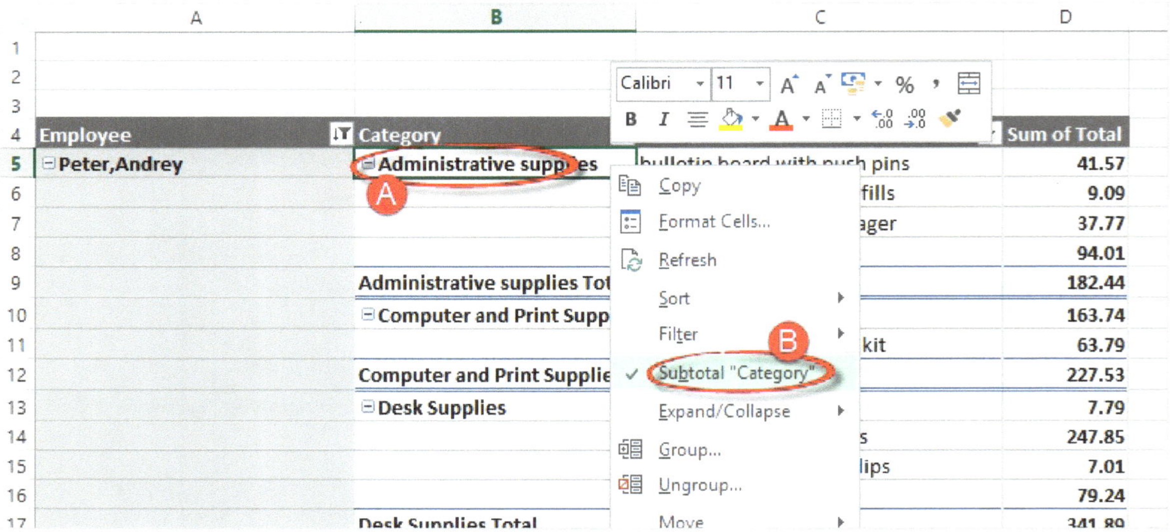

Fig. 45

After step B as illustrated in the figure above, your pivot table will look like fig. 46.

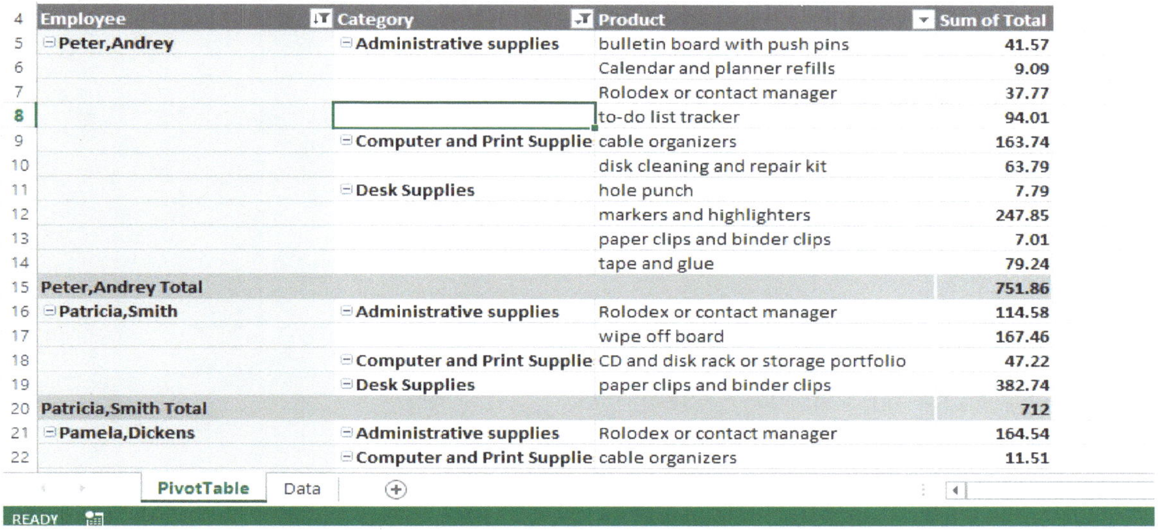

	Employee	Category	Product	Sum of Total
4	Employee	Category	Product	Sum of Total
5	⊟Peter,Andrey	⊟Administrative supplies	bulletin board with push pins	41.57
6			Calendar and planner refills	9.09
7			Rolodex or contact manager	37.77
8			to-do list tracker	94.01
9		⊟Computer and Print Supplie	cable organizers	163.74
10			disk cleaning and repair kit	63.79
11		⊟Desk Supplies	hole punch	7.79
12			markers and highlighters	247.85
13			paper clips and binder clips	7.01
14			tape and glue	79.24
15	Peter,Andrey Total			751.86
16	⊟Patricia,Smith	⊟Administrative supplies	Rolodex or contact manager	114.58
17			wipe off board	167.46
18		⊟Computer and Print Supplie	CD and disk rack or storage portfolio	47.22
19		⊟Desk Supplies	paper clips and binder clips	382.74
20	Patricia,Smith Total			712
21	⊟Pamela,Dickens	⊟Administrative supplies	Rolodex or contact manager	164.54
22		⊟Computer and Print Supplie	cable organizers	11.51

PivotTable   Data   (+)

READY

Fig. 46

5. *Remove the grand total through the design tab of the PivotTable tools, select grand total from layout and then select Off for rows and columns.*

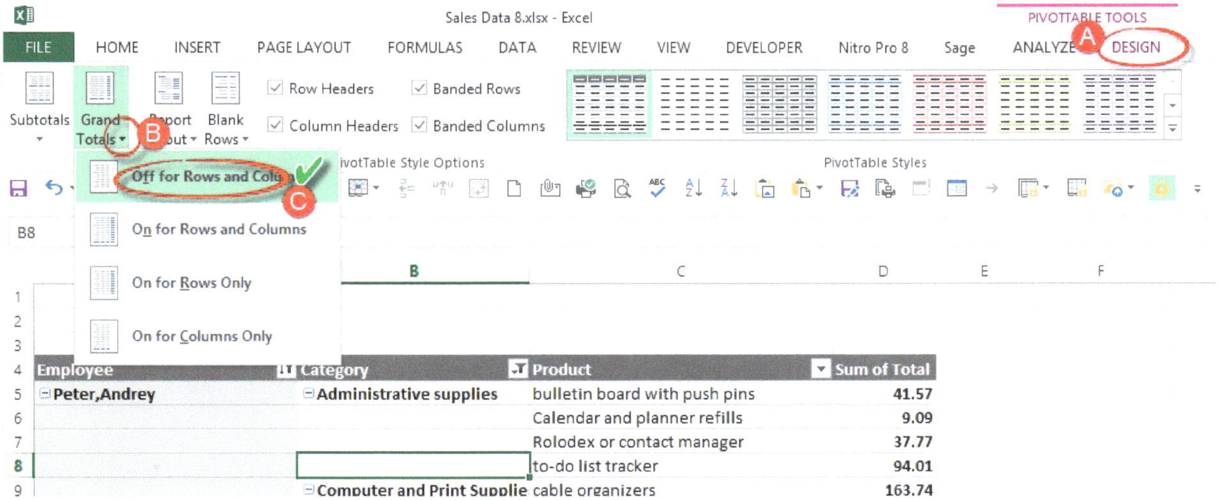

Fig. 47

After step C as illustrated in the figure above, your pivot table will look like fig. 48.

	A	B	C	D	E
1					
2					
3					
4	**Employee** 🔽	**Category** 🔽	**Product** 🔽	**Sum of Total**	
5	⊟ Peter,Andrey	⊟ Administrative supplies	bulletin board with push pins	41.57	
6			Calendar and planner refills	9.09	
7			Rolodex or contact manager	37.77	
8			to-do list tracker	94.01	
9		⊟ Computer and Print Supplies	cable organizers	163.74	
10			disk cleaning and repair kit	63.79	
11		⊟ Desk Supplies	hole punch	7.79	
12			markers and highlighters	247.85	
13			paper clips and binder clips	7.01	
14			tape and glue	79.24	
15	**Peter,Andrey Total**			**751.86**	
16	⊟ Patricia,Smith	⊟ Administrative supplies	Rolodex or contact manager	114.58	
17			wipe off board	167.46	
18		⊟ Computer and Print Supplies	CD and disk rack or storage portfolio	47.22	
19		⊟ Desk Supplies	paper clips and binder clips	382.74	
20	**Patricia,Smith Total**			**712**	
21	⊟ Pamela,Dickens	⊟ Administrative supplies	Rolodex or contact manager	164.54	
22		⊟ Computer and Print Supplies	cable organizers	11.51	
23			compressed air cannister for cleaning	23.77	
24	**Pamela,Dickens Total**			**199.82**	
25					

Fig. 48

6. *Save your work as Sales Data -9*

How to display multiple summations within a single pivot table

This is very useful when you need to display different summations such as: Total, Sum Average on a single pivot table.

1. *Open Sales Data -9 from your folder if it is not already open.*

2. *Remove the Category and product fields from the Row Labels list and add two more Totals fields to the values field. Your work will look similar to fig. 49.*

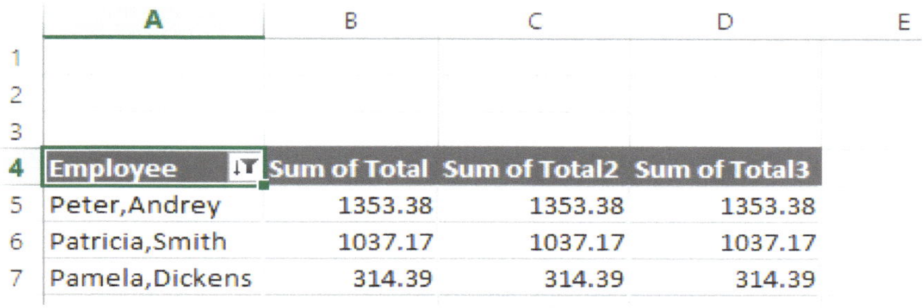

	A	B	C	D	E
1					
2					
3					
4	Employee	Sum of Total	Sum of Total2	Sum of Total3	
5	Peter,Andrey	1353.38	1353.38	1353.38	
6	Patricia,Smith	1037.17	1037.17	1037.17	
7	Pamela,Dickens	314.39	314.39	314.39	

Fig. 49

3. *Change the new totals to show Average Sales and Maximum sales for each employee by right clicking anywhere in column C then clicking on Value Field Settings on the shortcut menu.*

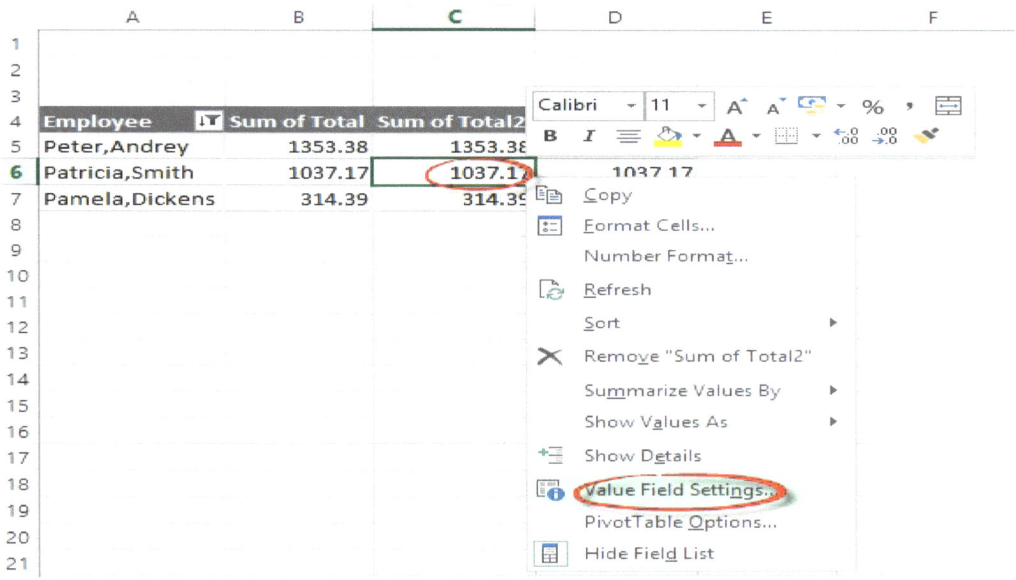

Fig. 50

4. *Select Average in the Summarize value field by list and use the same technique to make the Sum of Total 3 field display the maximum (Max) value. See fig. 51.*

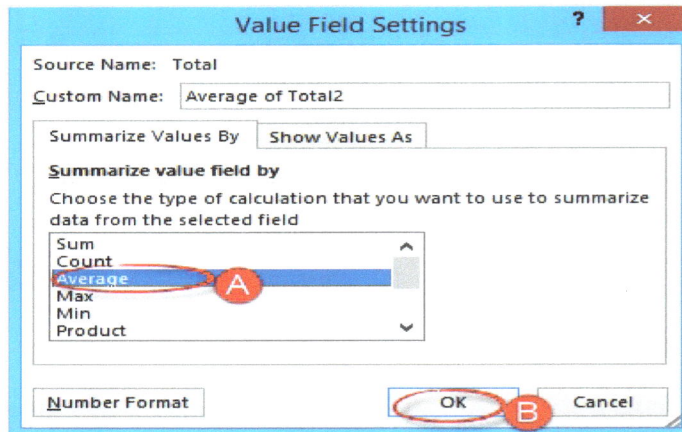

Fig. 51

After step B in the figure above, your pivot table will look like a figure similar to the one below

Fig. 52

5. *Add the grand total through the Design tab of the Pivot Tables tools and by selecting the grand total > On rows and Columns from the Layout section.*

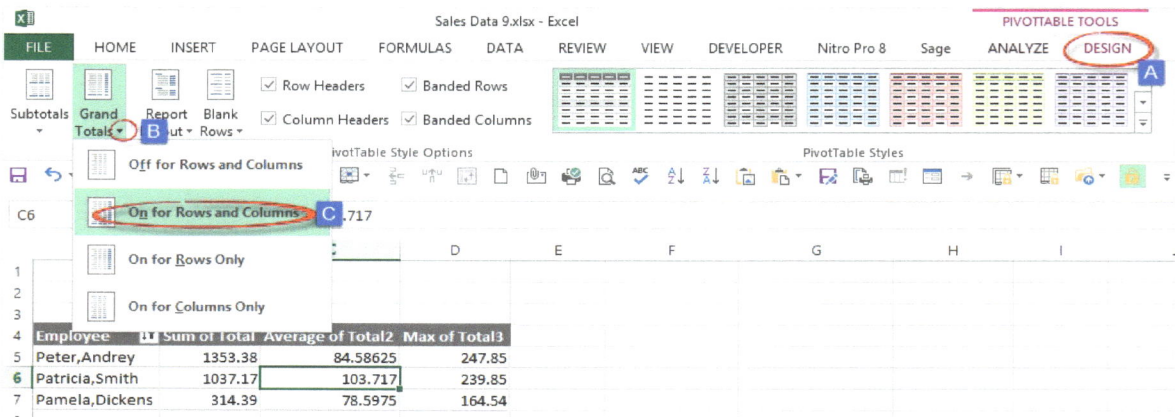

Fig. 53

After step C as illustrated in the figure above, your pivot table will look like the figure below

	A	B	C	D
1				
2				
3				
4	**Employee**	**⏏ Sum of Total**	**Average of Total2**	**Max of Total3**
5	Peter,Andrey	1353.38	84.58625	247.85
6	Patricia,Smith	1037.17	103.717	239.85
7	Pamela,Dickens	314.39	78.5975	164.54
8	**Grand Total**	**2704.94**	90.16466667	247.85

Fig. 54

6. *Save your work as Sales Data -10.*

How to add a calculated field to a pivot table

Say for example you wanted to calculate the bonus for the employees, here is how to go about doing it:

1. *Open the Sales Data -10 from your sample list folder.*

2. *Remove the Average & Max sales fields.*

3. *Format the Sum of Total Field to show a comma thousand separator.*

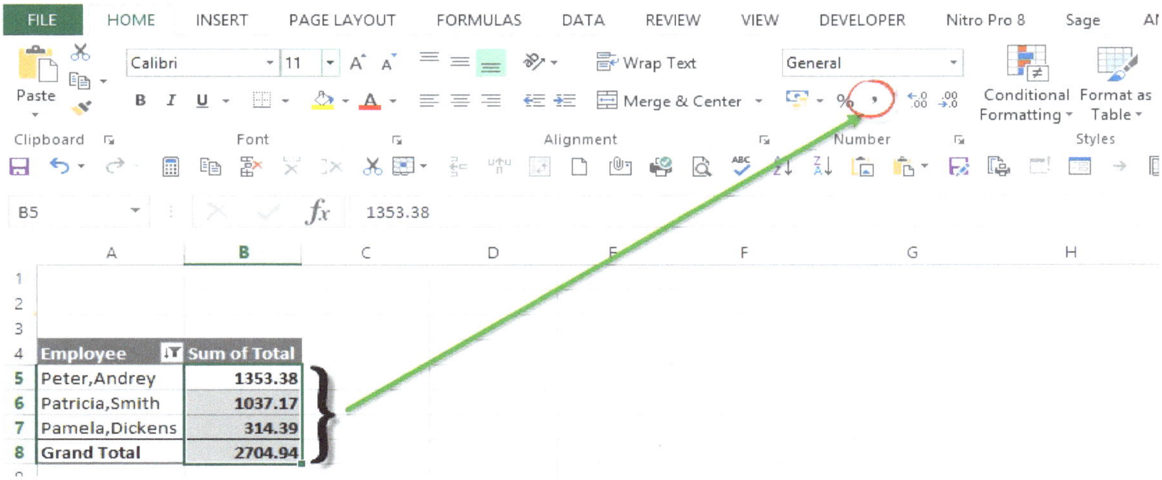

Fig. 55

4. *Now, to add a calculated field called Bonus that will calculate, say, 4% of total sales. Click* **on PivotTable Tools > Options > Tools > Formulas > Calculated Field.**

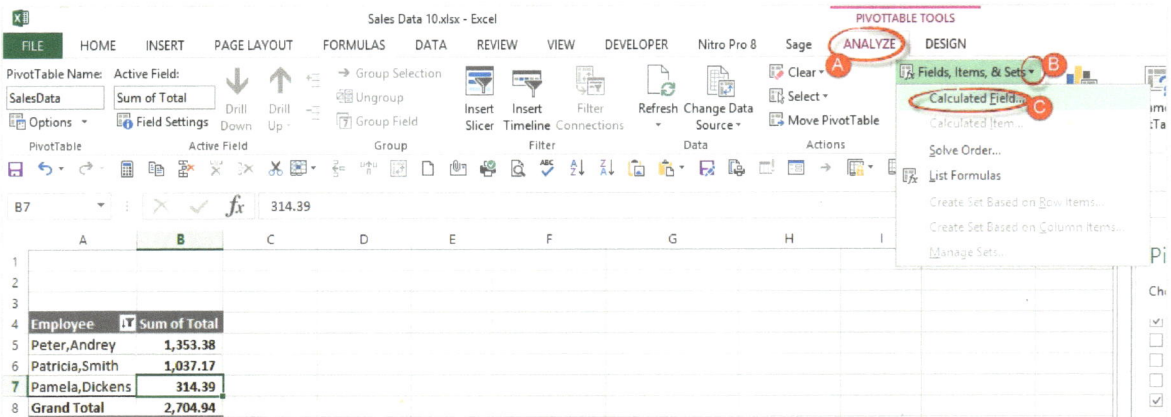

Fig. 56

5. Type **Bonus** *in the Name text box – See figure below.*

6. *Click in the Formula text box, remove the zero, leaving only the = sign, then Select Total in the Field list and then click the insert field button.*

7. *Type *4% to complete the formula and click OK button.*

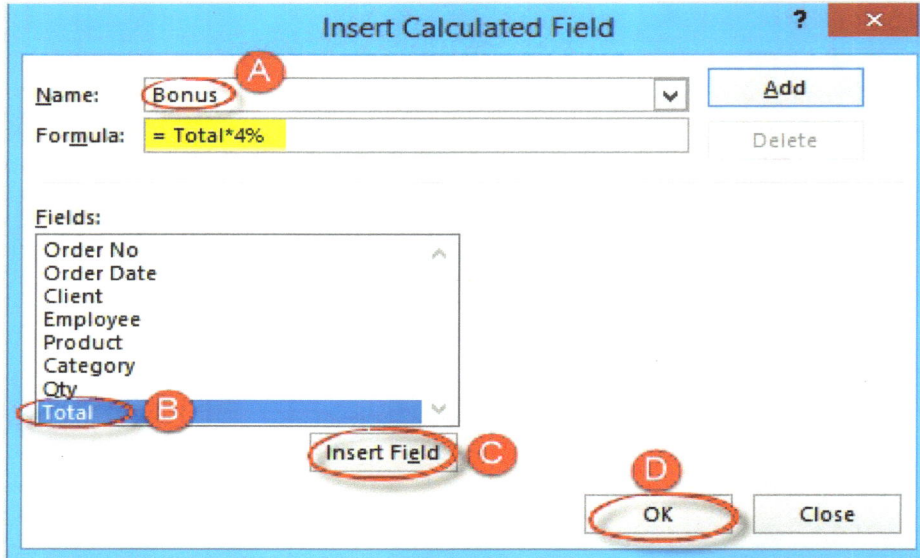

Fig. 57

8. *Remove the field header on row 4 by clicking: PivotTable Tools > Analyze> Show/Hide > Field headers.*

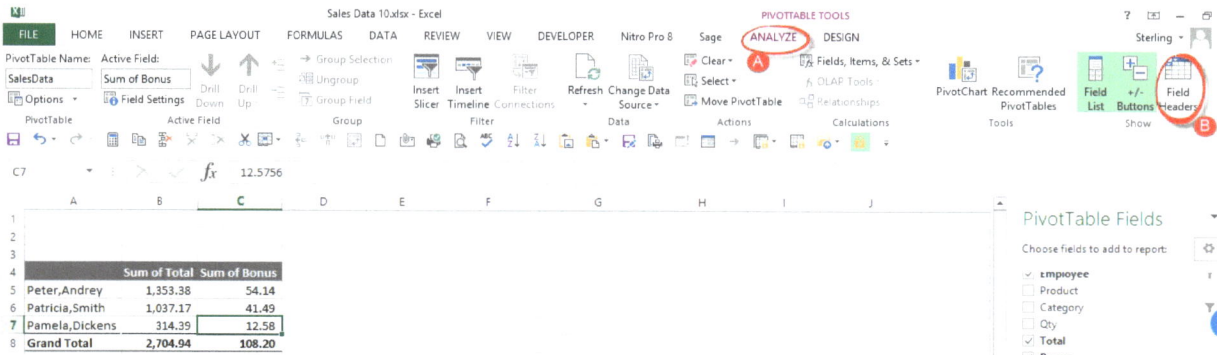

Fig. 58

9. *Save your work as Sales Data -11*

How to add a calculated item to a pivot table

In your role as the Accountant in your organization, sometimes you'll want to perform a calculation upon a selected number of items within a pivot table field. Say, for example, you are interested in the total sales for the Mailing, Marketing and Paper Supplies.

Calculated items provide a solution to this problem. We are going to add a calculated item to find out the total sales in these categories.

1. *Open Sales Data -11 from your file folder and clear all the filters by following steps A-C as shown in the figure below.*

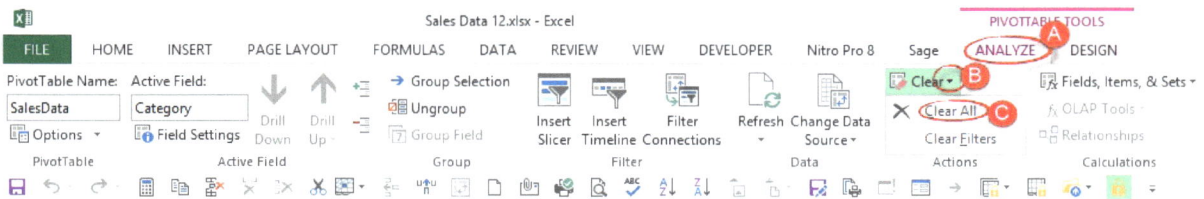

Fig. 59a

2. *On the Row label – drag the Category field and in the Values - Total field and format the Sum of Total to show two decimal places with a thousand comma separator.*

3. *Now, add a calculated item to show total sales for the categories: Mailing, Marketing and Paper supplies by clicking: PivotTable Tools >Analyze > Fields, Items & Sets> Calculated Item.*

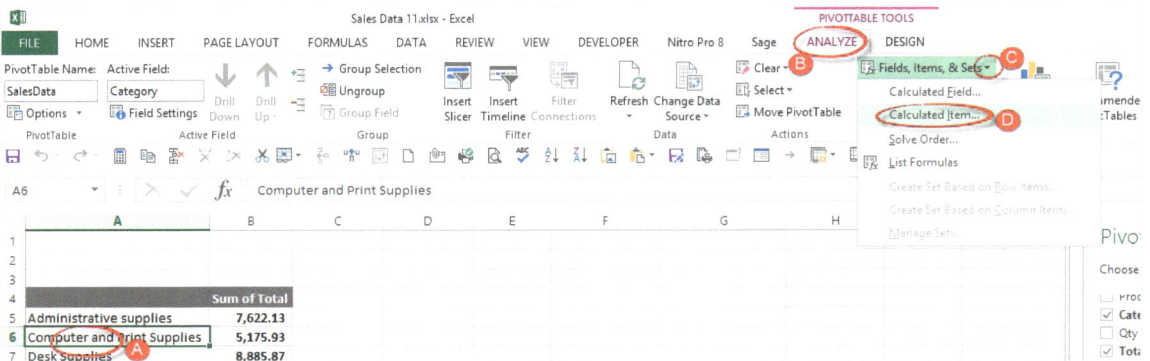

Fig. 59b

The insert Calculated Item dialog window appears after step D as illustrated in the figure above.

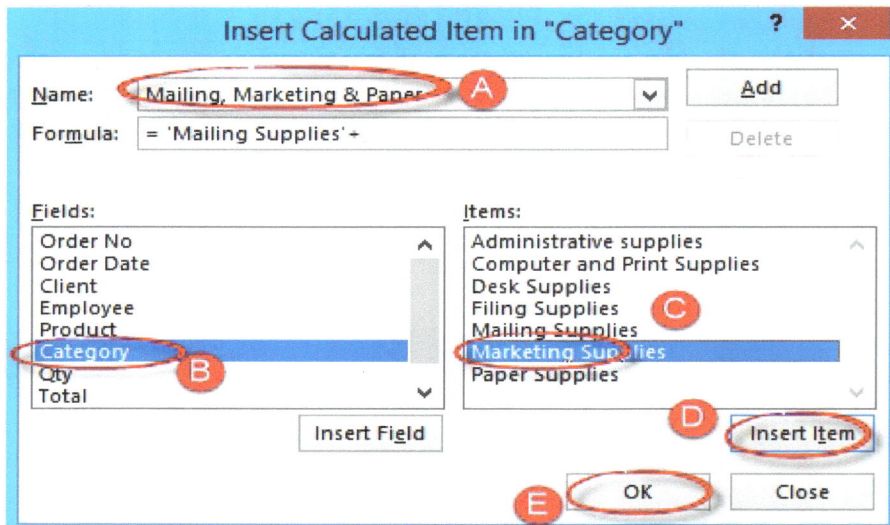

Fig. 60

4. *Name the calculated item:* **Mailing, Marketing & Paper.**

5. *Select the Category field and Mailing item and then click the insert item button.*

6. *Type the addition sign (+).*

7. *Add the marketing and paper supplies as in 5 above and click OK button. A total for Mailing, Marketing and Paper supplies appears at the bottom of the pivot table*

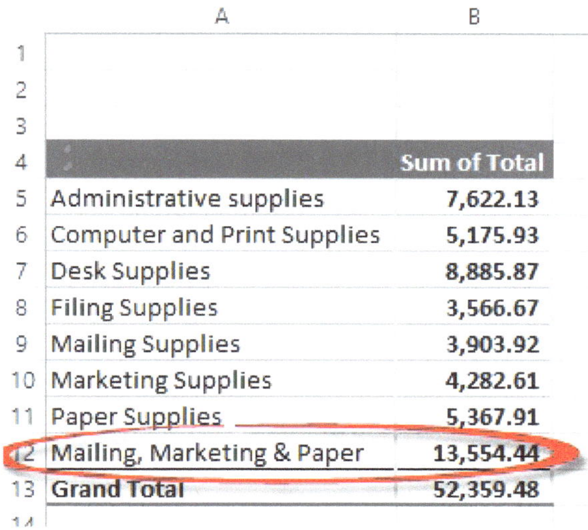

Fig. 61

8. *Filter the individual Mailing, Marketing and paper supplies so that they are no longer shown or included in the grand total, otherwise they will be double counted.* **We can use the slicer function for this – See below.**

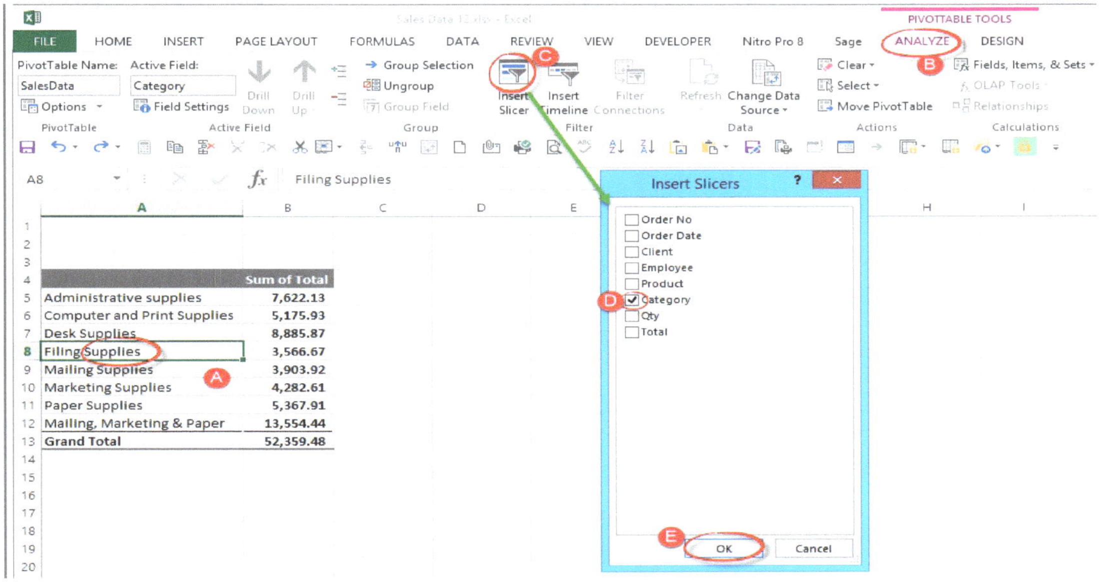

Fig. 62

After step E as illustrated in the figure above, the slicer for category will appear – see fig. 63.

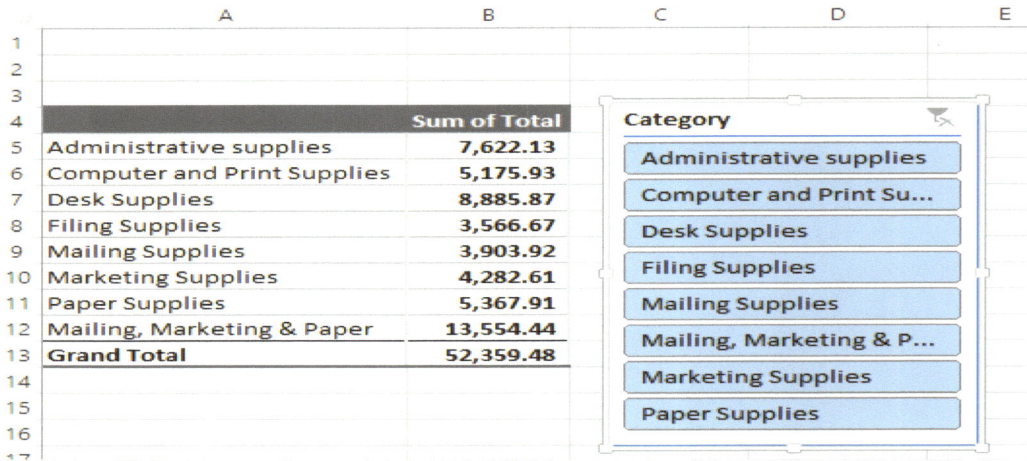

Fig. 63

9. *First click on Administrative Supplies on the slicer to select it, then hold down the Ctrl button on your computer keyboard, then select to select Computer and print supplies, Desk Supplies, Filing supplies and {Mailing, Marketing & Paper}, then release the Ctrl button on your computer keyboard – See figure below.*

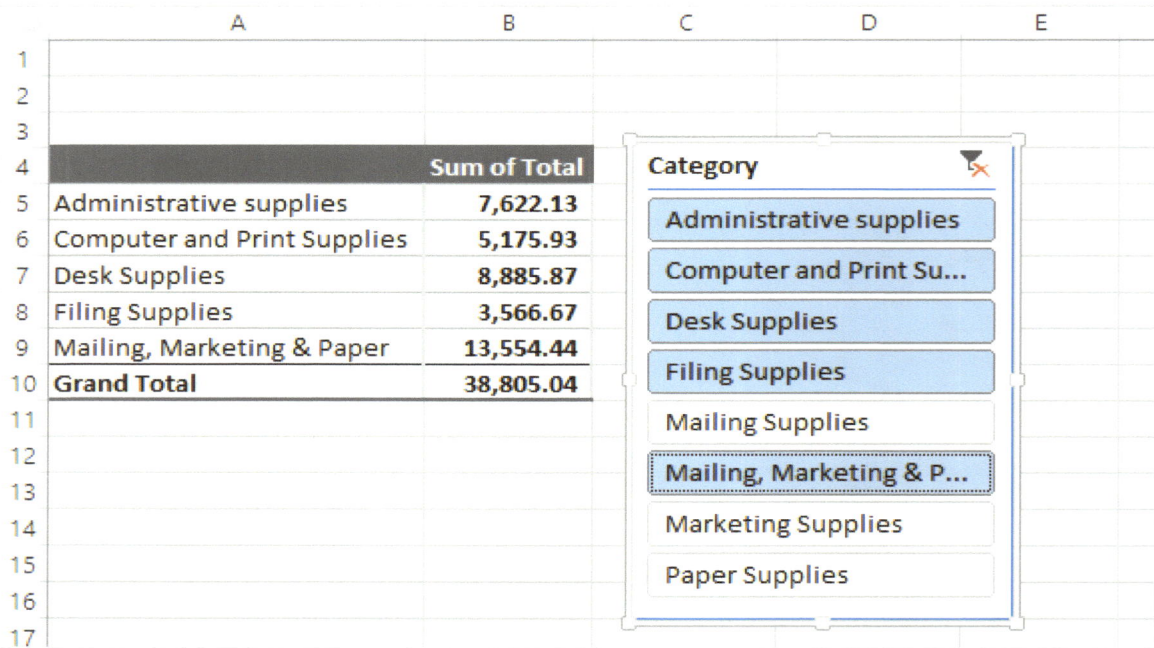

Fig. 64

10. *Save your work as Sales Data -12.*

How to group by Text

Here, we are going to show group totals for categories grouped in two's, two's & three's, i.e., Administrative, Computer & Print group; Desk & filing group; Mailing, marketing and paper group.

1. *Open Sales Data -12 from your file folder.*

2. *Remove all the existing fields and filters from the table including the calculated item added. Click on PivotTable Tools > Analyze > Clear > Clear All.*

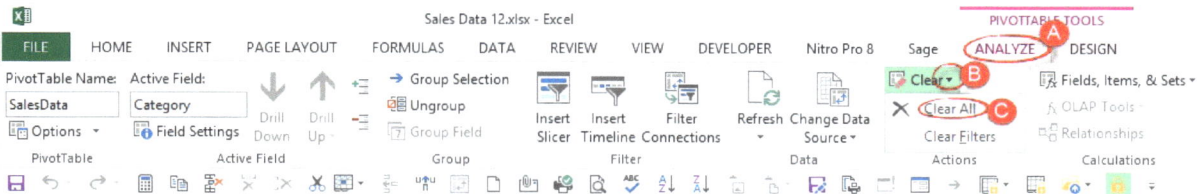

Fig. 65

For the slicer, clear it by right clicking on it and then selecting remove *Category* from the drop down that appears. See fig below.

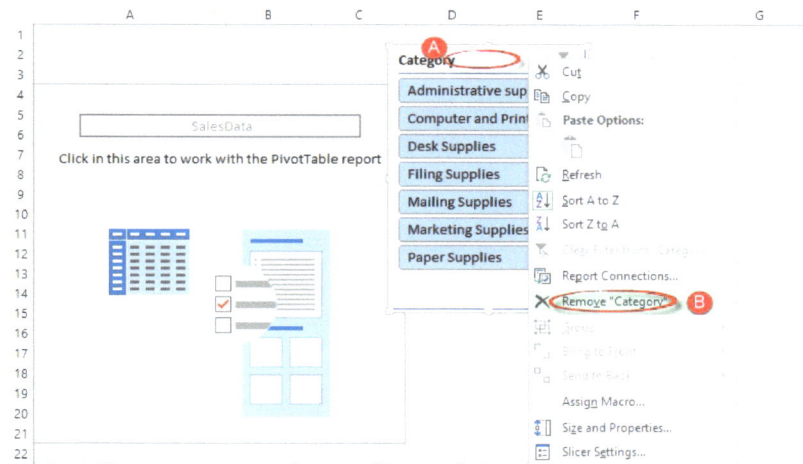

Fig. 66

3. *Now, add the following fields to the PivotTable: in Row column, add Category and in the Values column, add Qty.*

4. *Format the sum of quantity field so that it shows zero decimal places and a comma separator for thousands.*

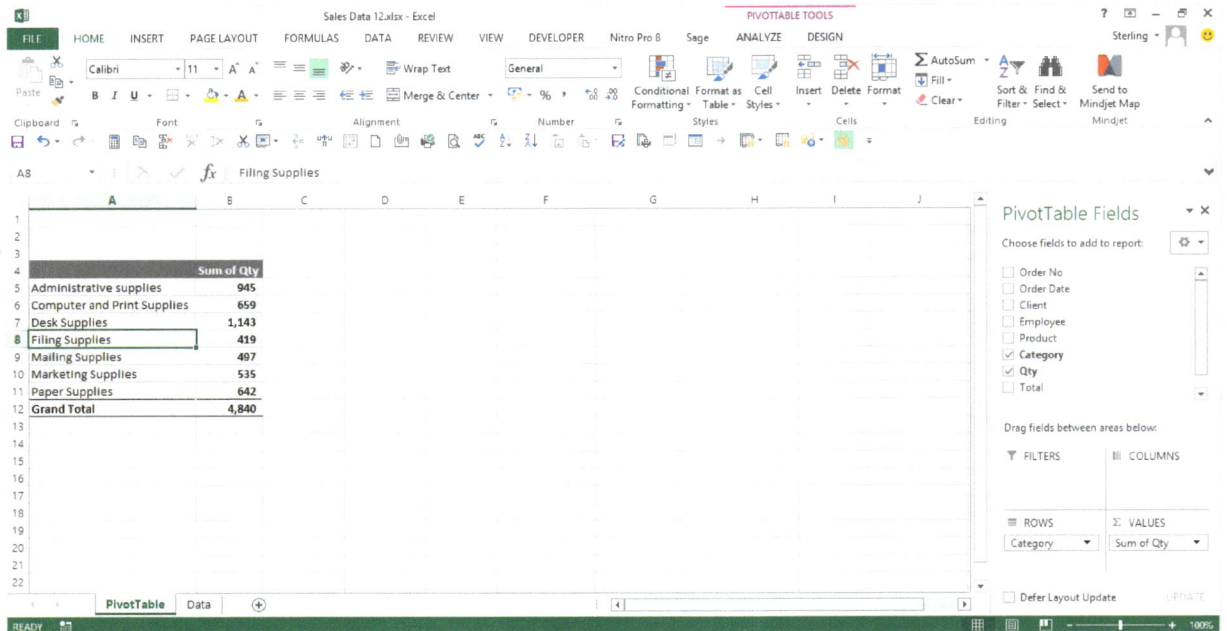

Fig. 67

5. Add a group for Administrative, Computer & Print supplies by: Clicking on the Administrative field in Column A- cell A5.

6. Hold down the <Ctrl> key and then click on Computer and Print Supplies –A6, in column A.

7. Right click on any of the selected fields and click Group in the shortcut menu that appears.

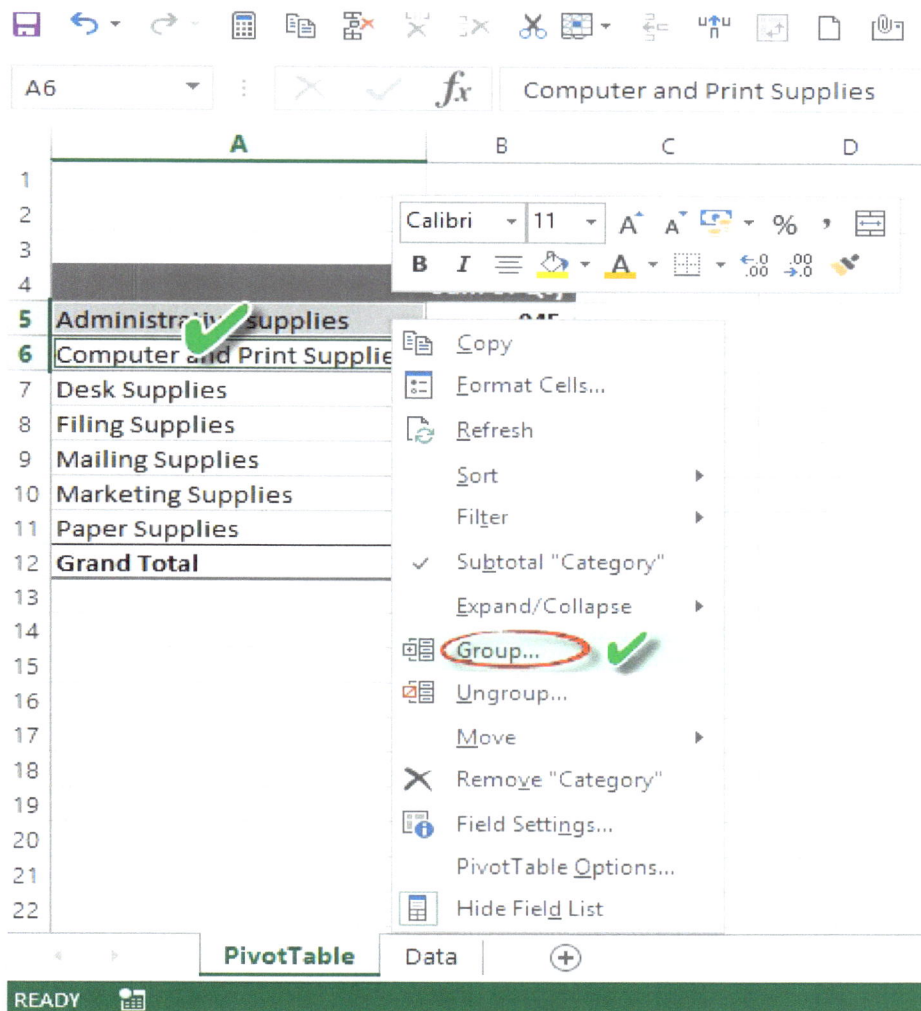

Fig. 68

8. *Change group 1 to Administrative, Computer & Printing supplies – See step A in fig. 69.*

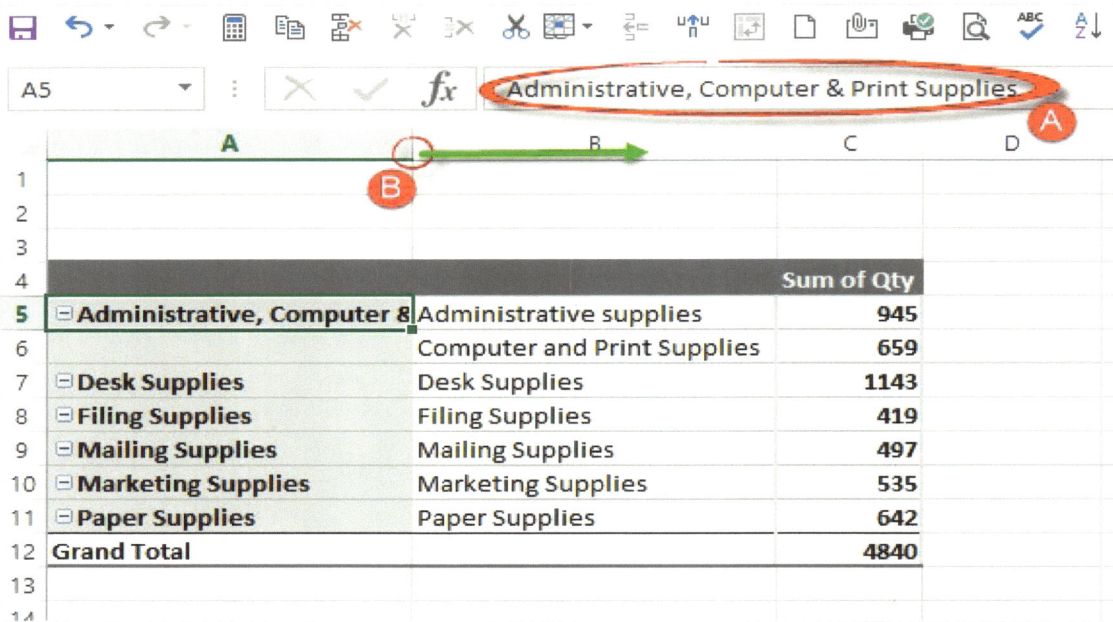

Fig. 69

9. *Create the Desk & Filing group and the Mailing, Marketing and Paper group in the same way as in 7 above.*

10. *Auto Size column A (See step B in the figure above) and collapse all Groups – click on the – sign for example in A5, A7 etc.*

Here is how your pivot table will look like after step 10.

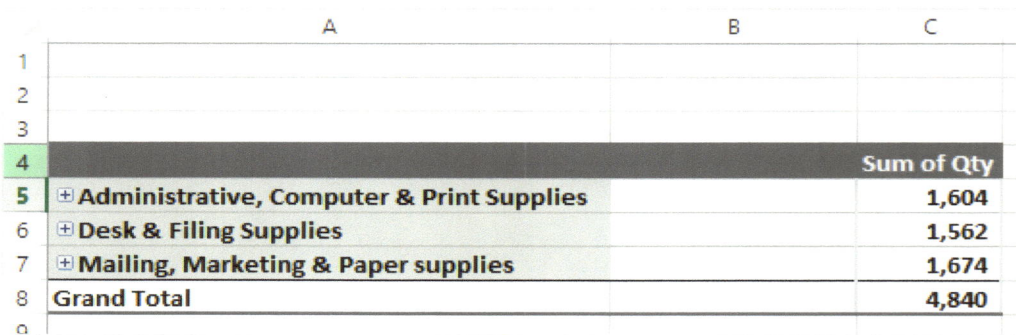

Fig. 70

11. *Add a subtotal for each group by Right clicking anywhere in column A, click on Fields settings from the shortcut menu that appears >Automatic option button in subtotals section > OK.*

12. *Expand category groups – click on the + sign in A5, A6 & A7.*

Here is how your pivot table now looks like.

		Sum of Qty
⊟ **Administrative, Computer & Print Supplies**	Administrative supplies	945
	Computer and Print Supplies	659
Administrative, Computer & Print Supplies Total		**1,604**
⊟ **Desk & Filing Supplies**	Desk Supplies	1,143
	Filing Supplies	419
Desk & Filing Supplies Total		**1,562**
⊟ **Mailing, Marketing & Paper supplies**	Mailing Supplies	497
	Marketing Supplies	535
	Paper Supplies	642
Mailing, Marketing & Paper supplies Total		**1,674**
Grand Total		**4,840**

Fig. 71

13. *Save your work as Sales Data – 13.*

How to group Items in the pivot table by date

1. *Open Sales Data -13 from your file folder if it is not already open.*

2. *Now, add the following fields into the pivot table: To Column label, add Order date; To Row Label, add Employee; and to Values label, add Total. Sales are now summarized by day.*

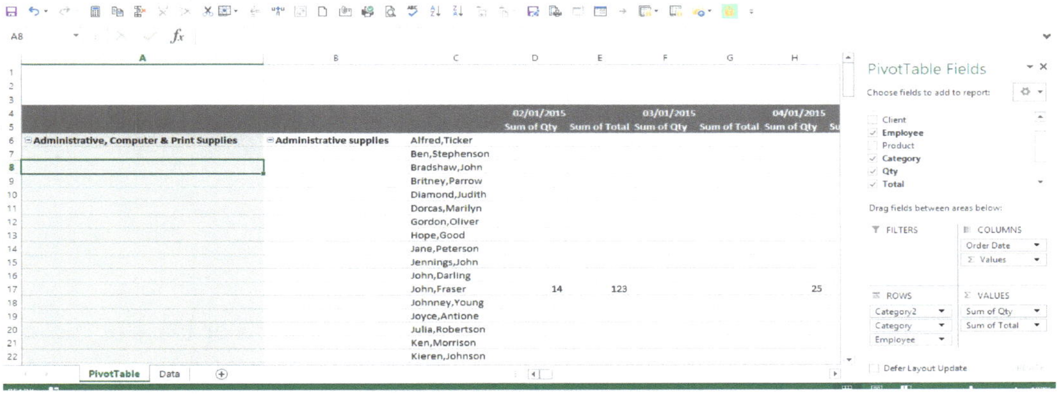

Fig. 72

3. *Now, show sales by month for each employee. You do this by: Right click on any of the dates in row 4, then*

click on Group on the shortcut menu that appears. A grouping dialog window appears. Select Months and Years. Click OK.

Now, click on any of the months in row 5, then click on Analyze from the Pivot table tools, then select insert timeline. In the dialogue box that appears, tick the order date check box and click OK - See figure below.

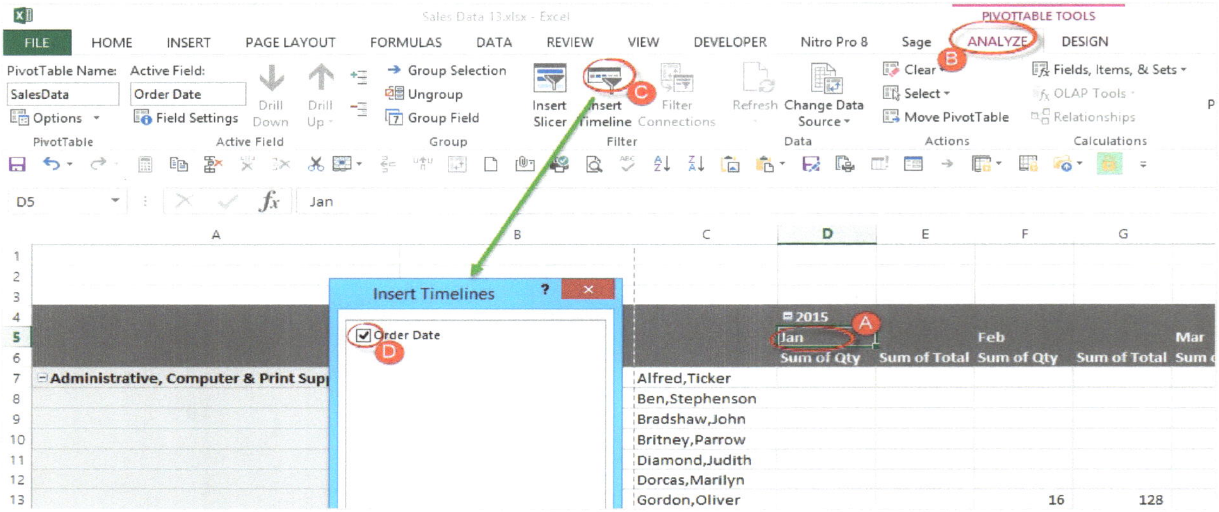

Fig. 73

After step E as illustrated in the figure above, you will then see the Timeline window – see figure below.

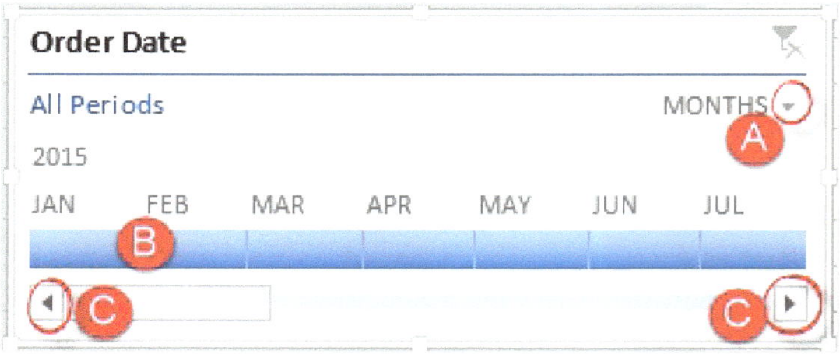

Fig. 74

You can choose whether you want to see report by: Years, Quarter, Months or Days of the month – just click the down arrow as illustrated in A in the figure above.

You can also select to see the report for on specific Years, Months, Quarters or specific days of the month by selecting them in the area marked B as illustrated in the figure above. You can move back &

forth in the time line to make your choices for B using scroll options – C. Check it out.

4. *From your timeline show in the pivot table sales for Jan & Feb 2015 for each employee – See figure below for your final result.*

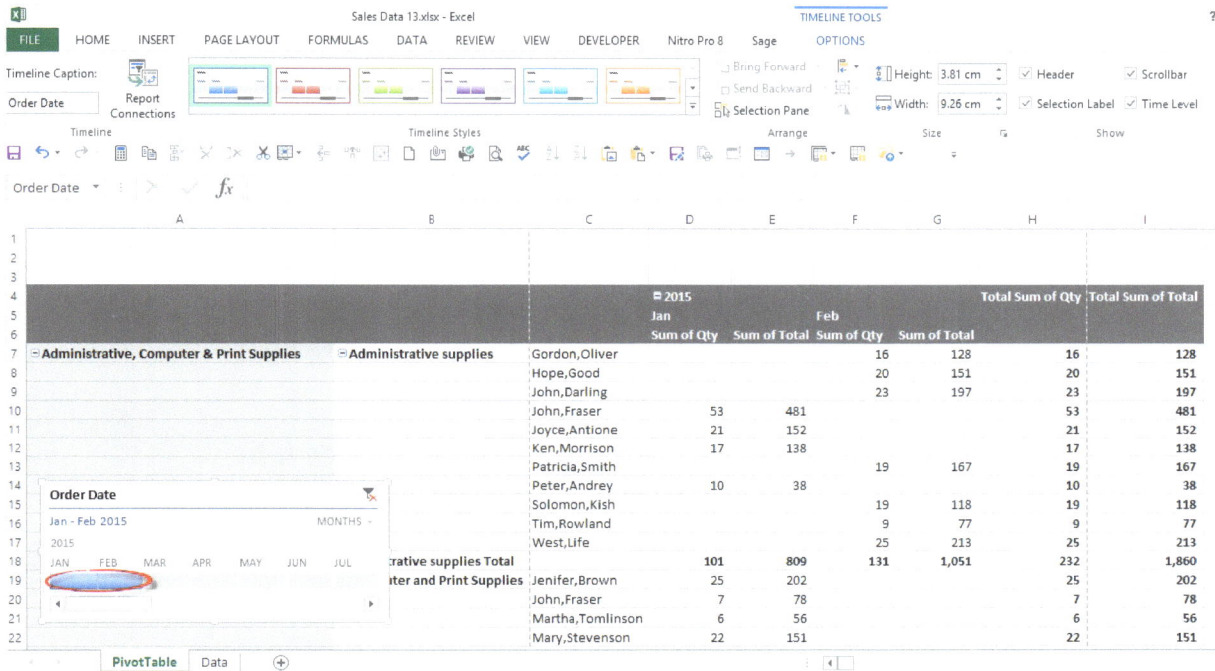

Fig. 75

5. *Save your work as Sales Data – 14.*

How to show row data by percentage of total rather than value

Sometimes when you are analysing sales data, you will be more interested in the percentage sales by the sales staff for each of the categories of the products your company sells.

Let's assume you are interested in finding out which category each employee is best at selling in order to enable the company to allocate sales leads for each category to the most competent sales person in that category. How will you do it?

Let's get to business, shall we?

1. *Open Sales data -14 from your file folder and remove all the existing fields, filters and filters from the pivot table (You learned how to do this already from previous workings).*

2. *Add the following fields to the pivot table: To the Row label, add Employee and the Column label, add Category, while to the Values label, add Total.*

3. *Format the sum of Total to show two decimal places and a thousand comma separator.*

4. *Show values as a percentage of each row total by Right-clicking on any of the numerical values in the pivot table. Thereafter, click on **Value fields Settings** from the shortcut menu that appears. The **Value Field Settings** window appears.*

5. *Click the **Show Values** tab from the value fields window.*

6. *Select **% of row total** in Show values as drop down list and then click OK button.*

See figure below for step 4 – 6 above.

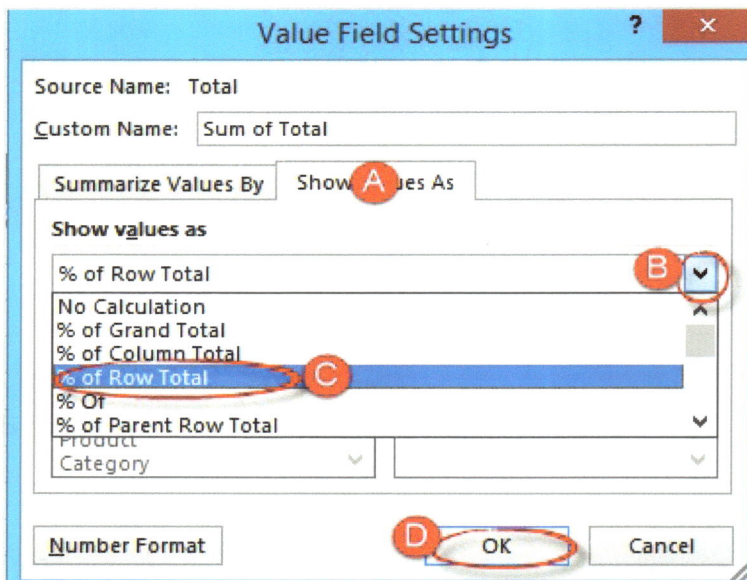

Fig. 76

Values are now shown as percentage of each employees' sales – see fig. 77.

Fig. 77

7. *Save your work as Sales Data -15.*

How to create a pivot chart from a pivot table

It is important to realize that a pivot chart always matches the data shown in the pivot table. Changes to the source data of the chart are made by modifying the pivot table underpinning it.

Let's see how this works:

1. *Open Sales Data -15 from your sample files and change the sum of total fields so that it displays values rather than percentage of total by following steps A-D in fig. 78 below.*

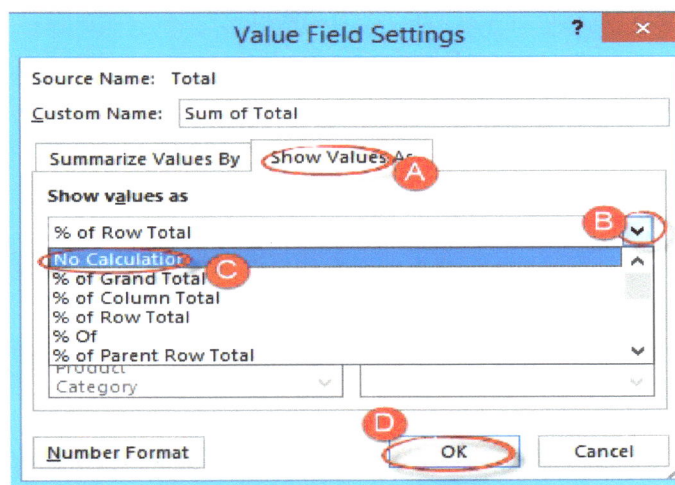

Fig. 78

After step D as illustrated in the figure above, your pivot table looks like figure below.

Sum of Total	Administrative supplies	Computer and Print Supplies	Desk Supplies	Filing Supplies	Mailing Supplies	
Alfred,Ticker	22.94	341.25		592.05	687.07	174.41
Ben,Stephenson	125.66	548.61		456.47	76.64	140.31
Bradshaw,John	125.87	292.11		33.77	143.27	19.1
Britney,Parrow	20.57	252.61		258.11	75.41	232.78
Davis,Davis		89.26		125.87	191.42	
Diamond,Judith	503.05	32.48		156.73	103.94	183.48
Dorcas,Marilyn	171.5			22.6	98.21	151.07
Evans,Gibbs		171.87		281.29	152.51	
Gordon,Oliver	197.8	174.23		265.53		272.88
Hope,Good	151.07			140.18		
Jane,Peterson	432.67	411.34		221.38		
Jenifer,Brown		202.36		170.71		185.24
Jennings,John	53.73			73.26		
John,Darling	388.4			282.69	106.02	238.85
John,Fraser	481.08	77.52				
Johnney,Young	372.97	29.66		182.34	169.58	
Joyce,Antione	152.33			214.9	88.74	

PivotTable   Data

Fig. 79

2. *Filter the pivot table so that the sales are only shown for these 4 employees: Alfred Ticker, Ben Stephenson, Bradshaw John and Britney Parrow. Use Slicer to filter employees. You learnt how to use slicer before see illustration in fig. 62.*

Fig. 80

3. *Create a clustered Column pivot chart from pivot table. You can do it by clicking anywhere in the pivot table to activate it, then clicking: PivotTable Tools > Analyze > Tools > Pivot Chart. The **Insert Chart** dialog window appears.*

4. *Click clustered column and the click Ok button.*

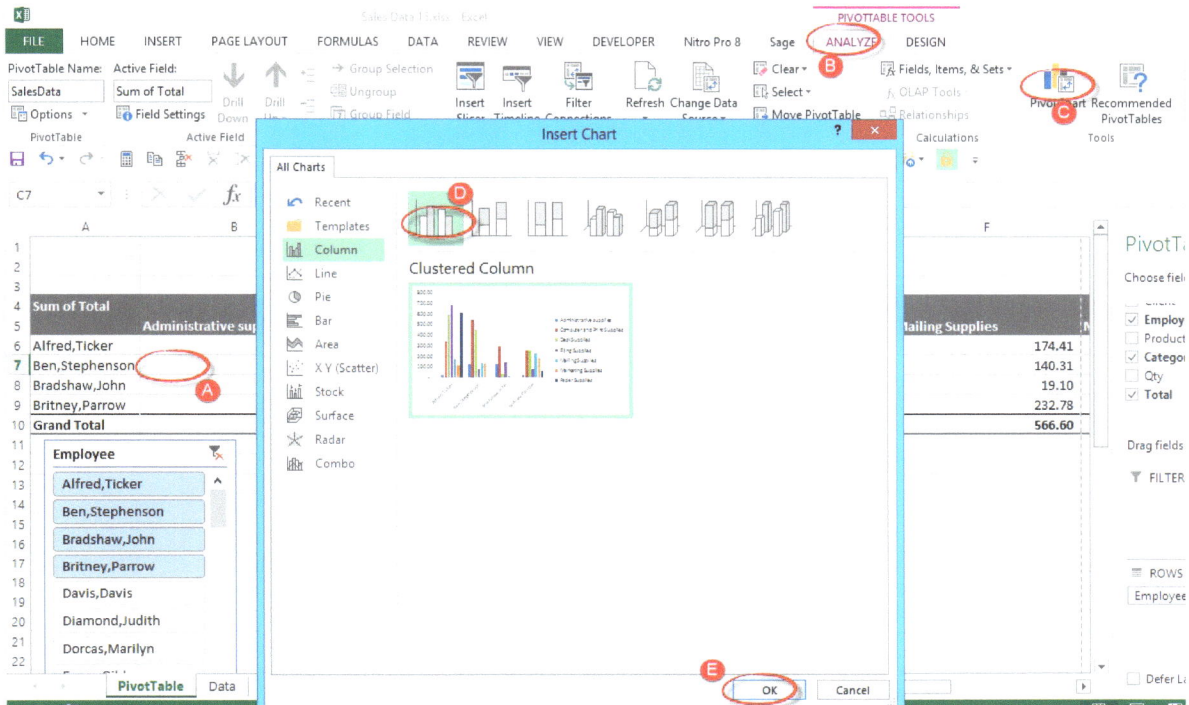

Fig. 81

5. *Move the chart to its own worksheet by; clicking on the chart to activate it, then click on PivotChart Tools > Design > Location > Move chart. The Move Chart dialog window appears.*

6. *In the dialog window type in **Employee sales 2015** into the new sheet box.*

7. *Click OK and you will notice that the chart now resides on its own sheet.*

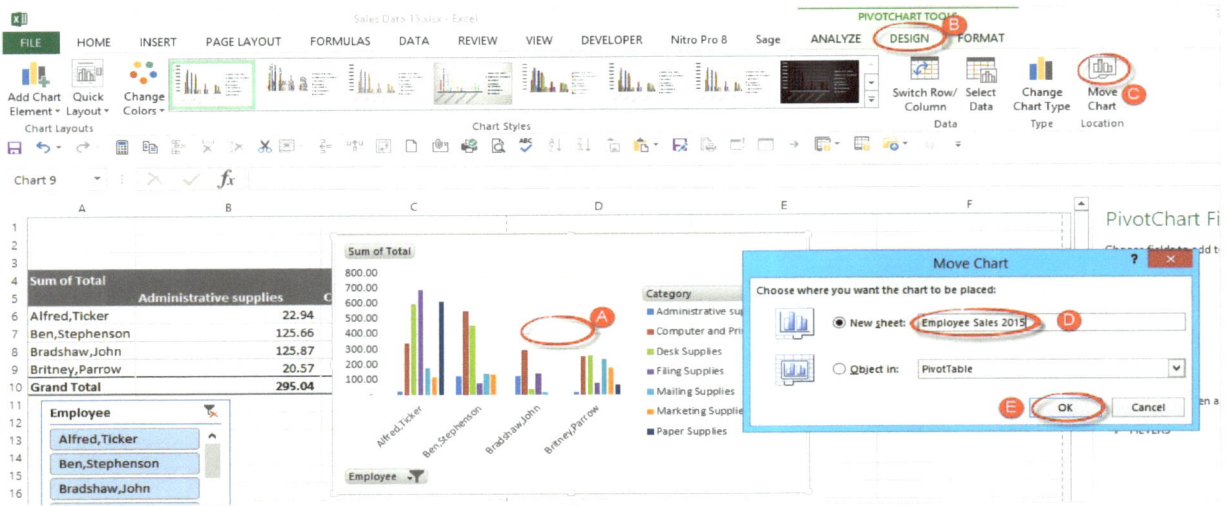

Fig. 82

After step E as illustrated in the figure above, this is how your work looks like – see *fig. 83* below.

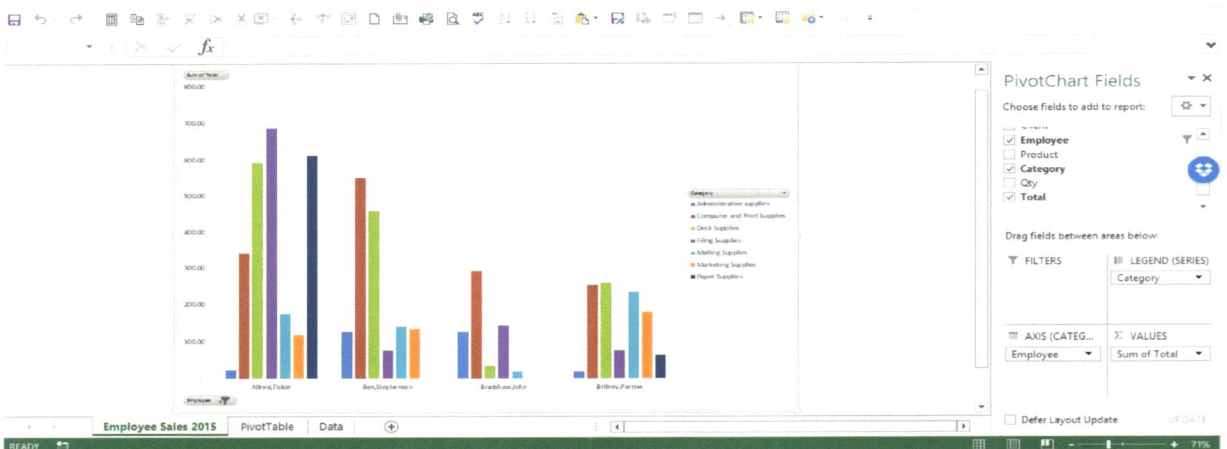

Fig. 83

8. *Save your work as Sales Data – 16.*

How to embed multiple pivot tables into a worksheet

I like seeing things in a summarised form, don't you too? Pivot Table is all about that, but what we are going to do now is take it to another level by having multiple pivot tables in one work sheet. How about that?

You are now going to create a sales summary by Client (How much did we get from each client in 2015), by Category (How much did each category bring in), by Employee (How did our staff do, how much did each sell). All this information we would like to see it in one page at a glance.

Let's do it!

1. *Open Sales Data -16 from your sample files and add a new work sheet and name it:* **Sales Summary 2015.**

2. *Type Sales Summary into Cell B2 and apply the Title style to it.*

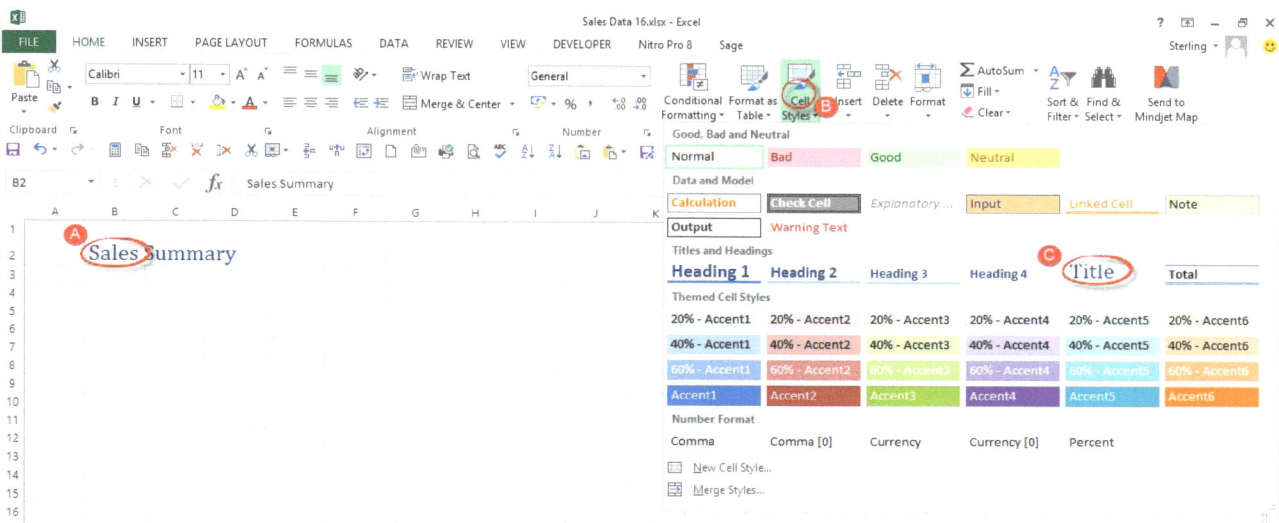

Fig. 84

3. *Embed the pivot table starting from cell B4. Click cell B4, then Click Insert > Pivot table.*

4. *Type Data into the Table/Range Box and click OK.*

5. *Show sales by Client by selecting Client in the Row field and Total in the Values field.*

6. *Embed a pivot table starting at cell B33 and show sales by Category.*

7. *Embed yet again another pivot table starting at cell E4 and show total sales by Employee.*

8. *Format all values to show two decimal places and thousand separators.*

9. *Add five rating (icon set) conditional format to cells C5:C30.*

10. *Add Green data bar conditional format to Cell C34:C40. Use the same approach as in 9 above making sure you chose the correct conditional format.*

11. *Do the same and add Green- Yellow-Red colour scales conditional format to cells F5:F42.*

Here is how your final multiple pivot Table report looks like – see *fig. 85* below.

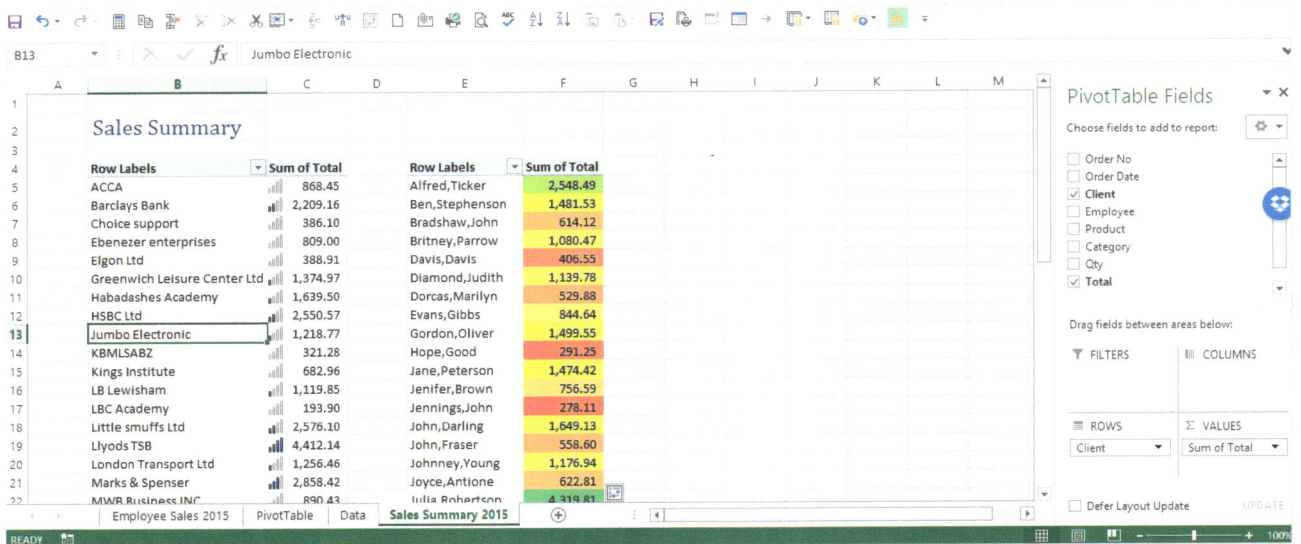

Fig. 85

12. *Save your work as Sales Data -17*

Congratulations! You are now A Pivot Table "Expert".

VLOOKUP

What is VLOOKUP?

Well, of course it's an Excel function. It is one of the <u>lookup and reference functions</u> in excel used when you need to find things in a table or a range by row. For example, look up an employee's last name by her employee number, or find her phone number by looking up her last name (just like a telephone book).

I am going to illustrate how you can use the VLOOK function on the assumption that you already have a passing understanding of Excel functions, and can use basic functions such as SUM, AVERAGE, and TODAY. In its most common usage, VLOOKUP is a database function, meaning that it works with database tables – or more simply, lists of things in an Excel worksheet.

What sort of things? Well, any sort of thing. You may have a worksheet that contains a list of employees, or products, or customers, or CDs in your CD collection, or stars in the galaxy. It doesn't really matter.

The secret to VLOOKUP is to organise your data so that the value you look up (for example employee's last name) is to the left of the return value you want to find (employee's phone number).

Let's just get on with it and look at this function in action.

Here's an example of a list, or database. In this case, it's a list of products that our fictitious company - Tristar stationers sells.

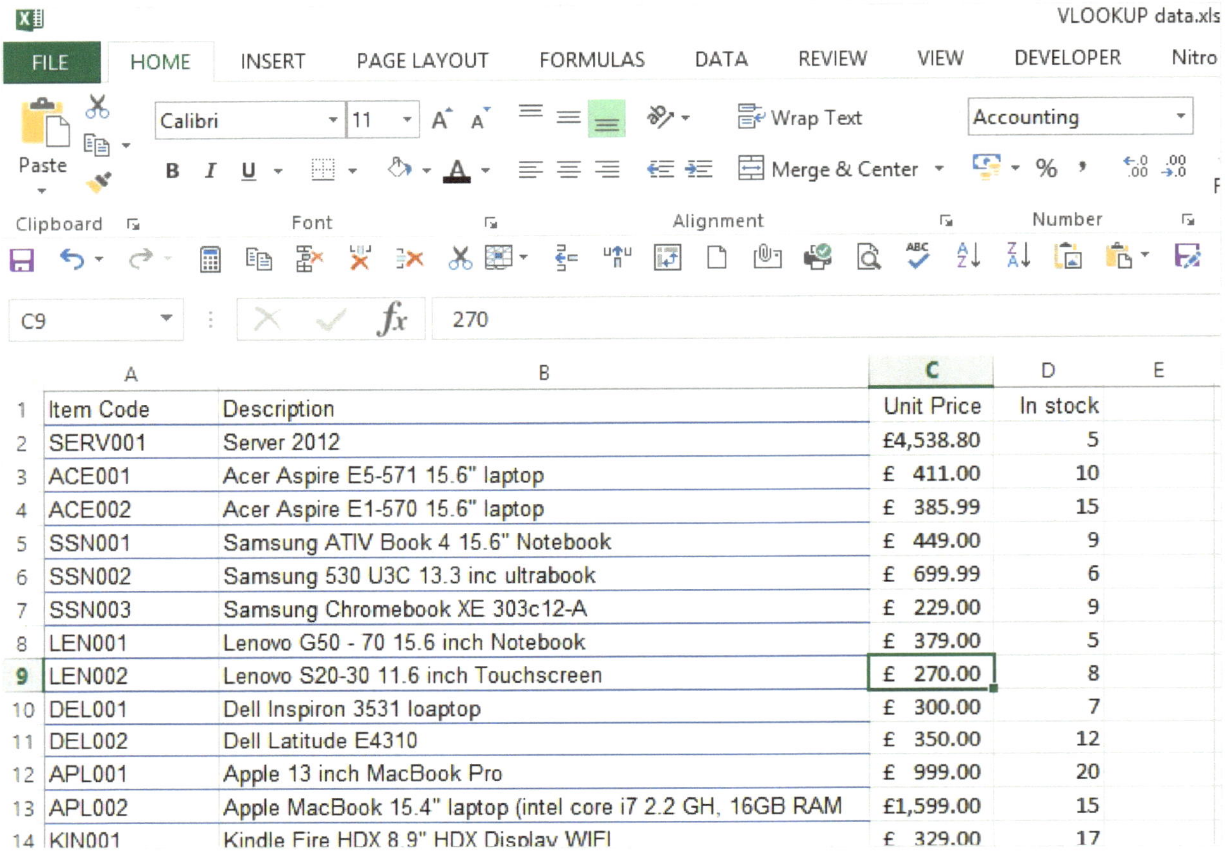

	A	B	C	D
1	Item Code	Description	Unit Price	In stock
2	SERV001	Server 2012	£4,538.80	5
3	ACE001	Acer Aspire E5-571 15.6" laptop	£ 411.00	10
4	ACE002	Acer Aspire E1-570 15.6" laptop	£ 385.99	15
5	SSN001	Samsung ATIV Book 4 15.6" Notebook	£ 449.00	9
6	SSN002	Samsung 530 U3C 13.3 inc ultrabook	£ 699.99	6
7	SSN003	Samsung Chromebook XE 303c12-A	£ 229.00	9
8	LEN001	Lenovo G50 - 70 15.6 inch Notebook	£ 379.00	5
9	LEN002	Lenovo S20-30 11.6 inch Touchscreen	£ 270.00	8
10	DEL001	Dell Inspiron 3531 loaptop	£ 300.00	7
11	DEL002	Dell Latitude E4310	£ 350.00	12
12	APL001	Apple 13 inch MacBook Pro	£ 999.00	20
13	APL002	Apple MacBook 15.4" laptop (intel core i7 2.2 GH, 16GB RAM	£1,599.00	15
14	KIN001	Kindle Fire HDX 8.9" HDX Display WIFI	£ 329.00	17

Fig. 86

Usually lists like this have some sort of unique identifier for each item in the list. In this case, the unique identifier is in the "Item Code" column.

Note: For the VLOOKUP function to work with a database/list, that list must have a column containing the unique identifier (or "key", or "ID"), and that column must be the first column in the table. Our sample database above satisfies this criterion.

The hardest part of using VLOOKUP is understanding exactly what it's for. So let's see if we can get that clear first:

VLOOKUP retrieves information from a database/list based on a supplied instance of the unique identifier.

Put another way, if you put the VLOOKUP function into a cell and pass it one of the unique identifiers from your database, it will return you one of the pieces of information associated with that unique identifier. In the example above, you would pass VLOOKUP an item code, and it would return to you either the corresponding item's description, its price, or its availability (its "In stock" quantity). Which of these pieces of information will it pass you back? Well, you get to decide this when you're creating the formula.

If all you need is one piece of information from the database, it would be a lot of trouble to go to construct a formula with a VLOOKUP function in it. Typically you would use this sort of functionality in a reusable spreadsheet, such as a template. Each time someone enters a valid item code, the system would retrieve all the necessary information about the corresponding item.

Let's create an example of this: An Invoice Template that we can reuse over and over in our fictitious company.

First we start Excel…

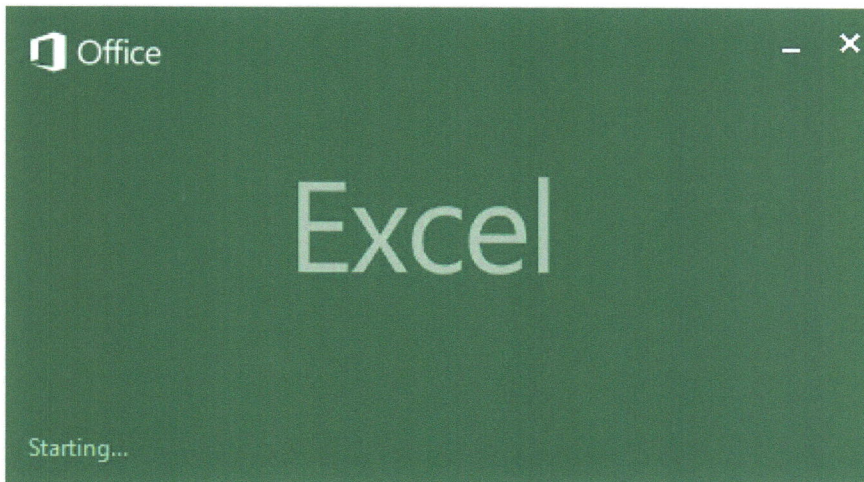

Fig. 87

… and we create ourselves a blank invoice: see figure below (you will have to create one from scratch). Make sure you resize cell B11 to make it a bit long and also make sure that you wrap text in it as illustrated in the figure below and do the same for cells B12-B19.

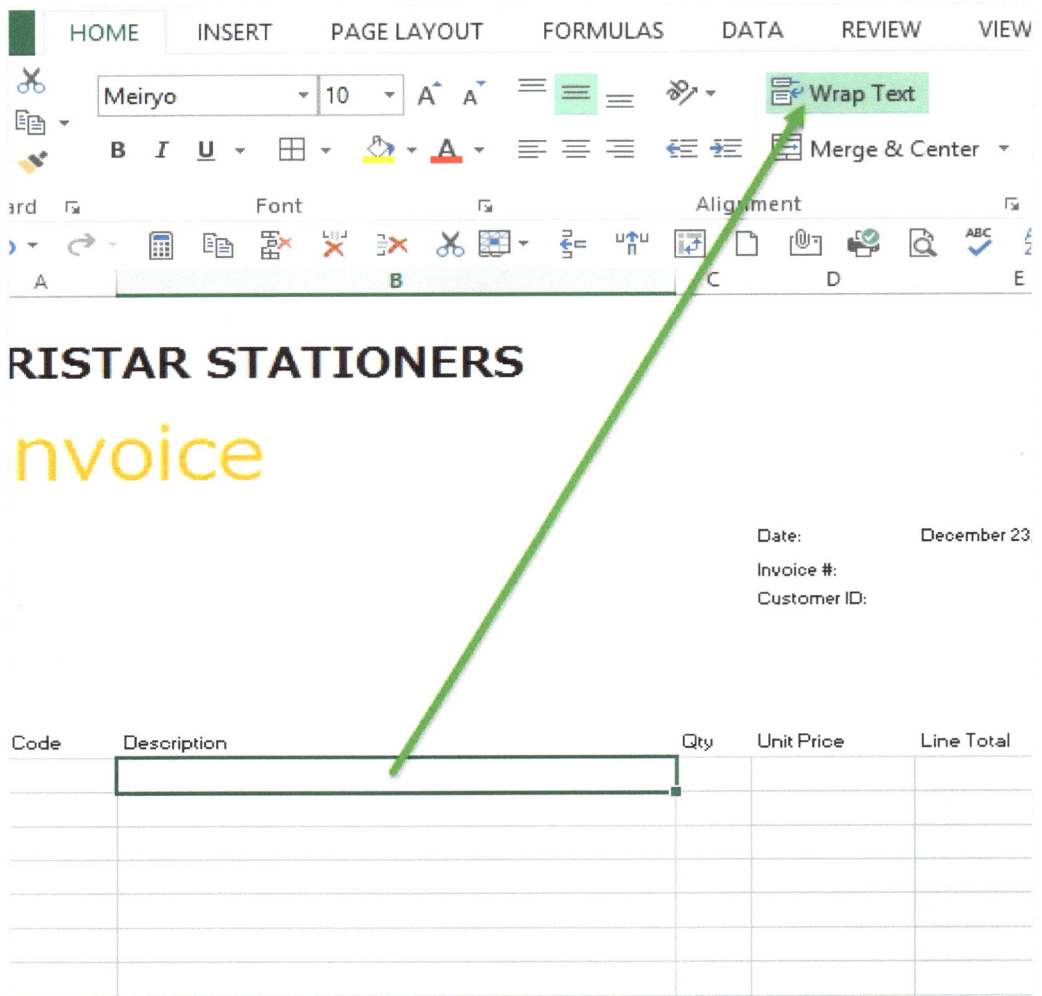

Fig. 88

Let's put some formulas in this invoice to help automate some tasks later.

In Cell E3, type in =NOW( ) or =TODAY( ) and then enter.

In cell E11, type in =C11*D11 and the press Enter.

Fig. 89

Incorporating "IF" & "ISBLANK" functions

Once you press Enter, you will see something similar to "0.00" if you have formatted the cell to 2 decimal places or you will simply see "0" in cell E11.

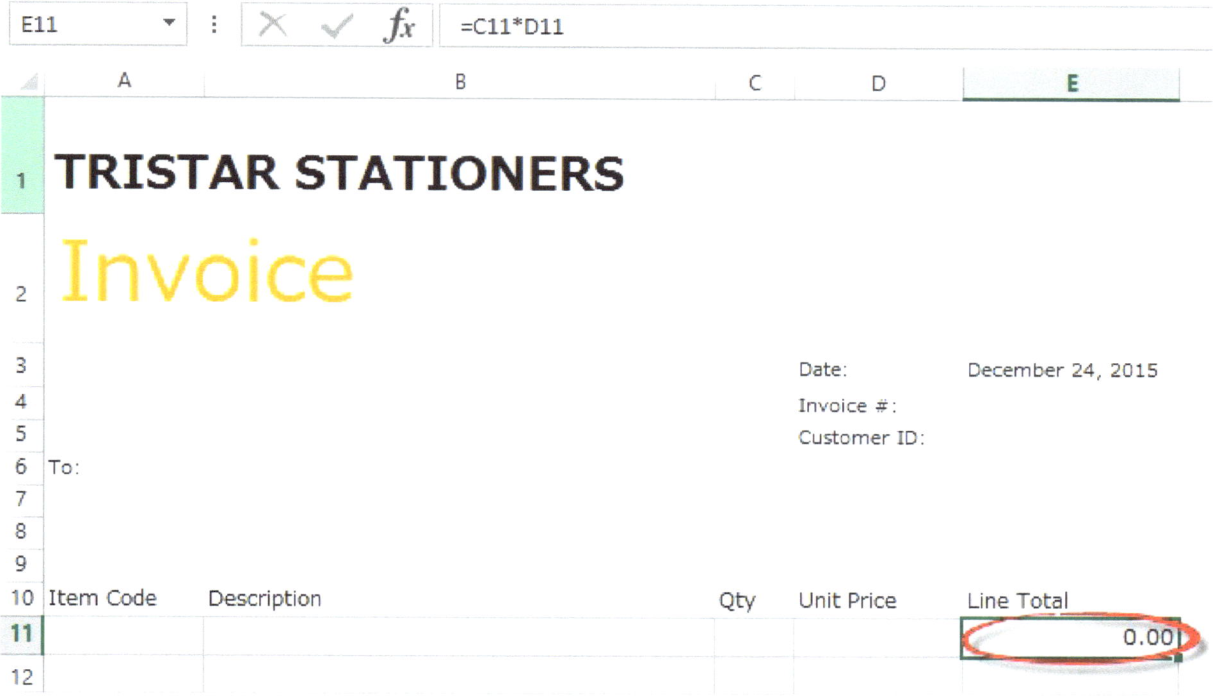

Fig. 90

Now, if you want to keep your invoice template tidy and don't want to see the 0.00 or the – sign on cell E11if there are no figures in cell C11 and or D11, you can use "ISBLANK" & "IF" function. Do this, in cell E11, type in =IF(ISBLANK(C11)," ",(C11*D11)). Another formula to use would be: =IF(C11="", "",(C11*D11))

What you are basically saying here is this "if cell C11 is blank, put nothing in cell E11, otherwise if there is something in cell C11, then multiply that with what is in cell D11.

Let's try it and see.

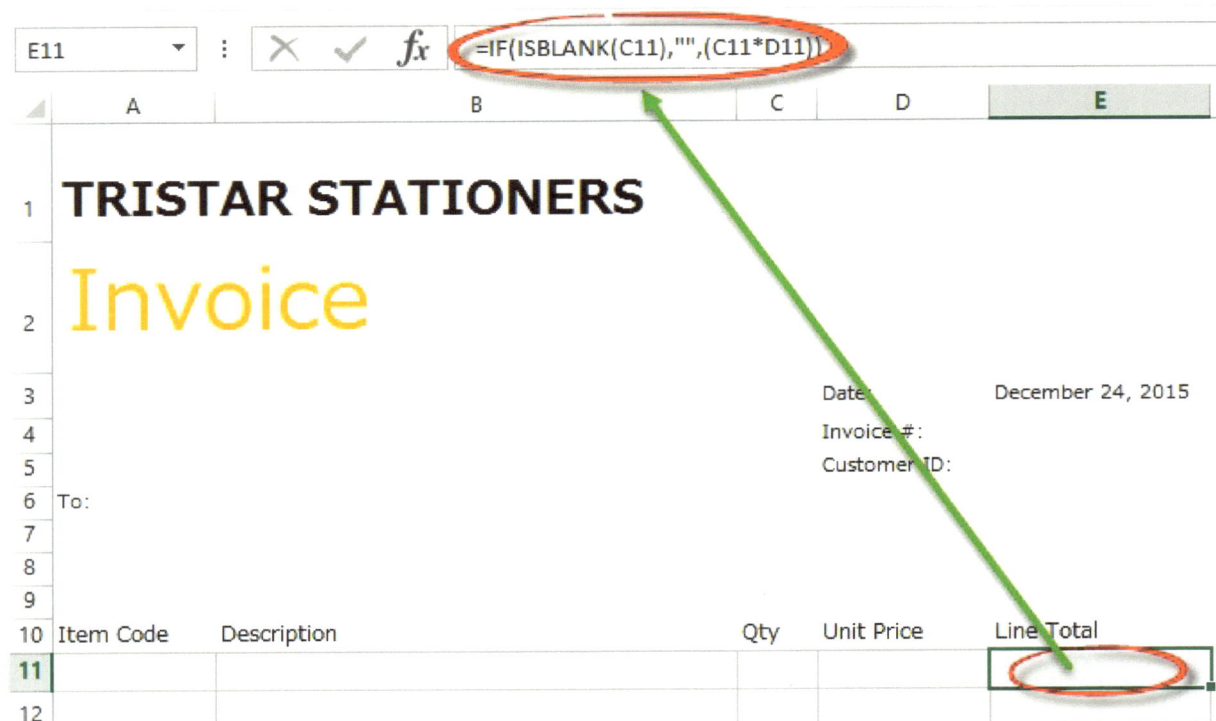

Fig. 91

Wala! The "0.00" and or "-", or "0"are gone from cell E11 because of the ISBLANK and IF function.

Click on the bottom right corner of cell E11 when you hoover over it and see the dark + sign. Now drag the click down up to cell E19 and release it – that will copy the formula to cell E12-E19.

Format cells E20 - E22 to show £ sign and in cell E20 type in the formula =SUM(E11:E19) and press enter, in cell E21 type in =E20*20% and press enter, and in cell E22 type in = SUM(E20:E21) and press enter.

You are now going to start using the VLOOKUP function!

The way this is going to work is this: You are going to fill the invoice template you have just created with a series of item codes in column "A" – starting from "A11", and the system will retrieve each item's description and price, which will be used to calculate the line total for each item (assuming we enter a valid quantity).

For the purposes of keeping this example simple, we will locate the product database on a separate sheet in the same workbook.

In reality, it's more likely that the product database would be located in a separate workbook. It makes little difference to the VLOOKUP function, which doesn't really care if the database is located on the same sheet, a different sheet, or a completely different workbook.

Now, open a new worksheet (call it Product Database) in the same workbook you have the blank invoice template and in cell A1- type in "Item Code" in cell B1- type in Description" in cell C1 – type in Unit price" and in cell D1 – type in – "In stock" (See figure below)

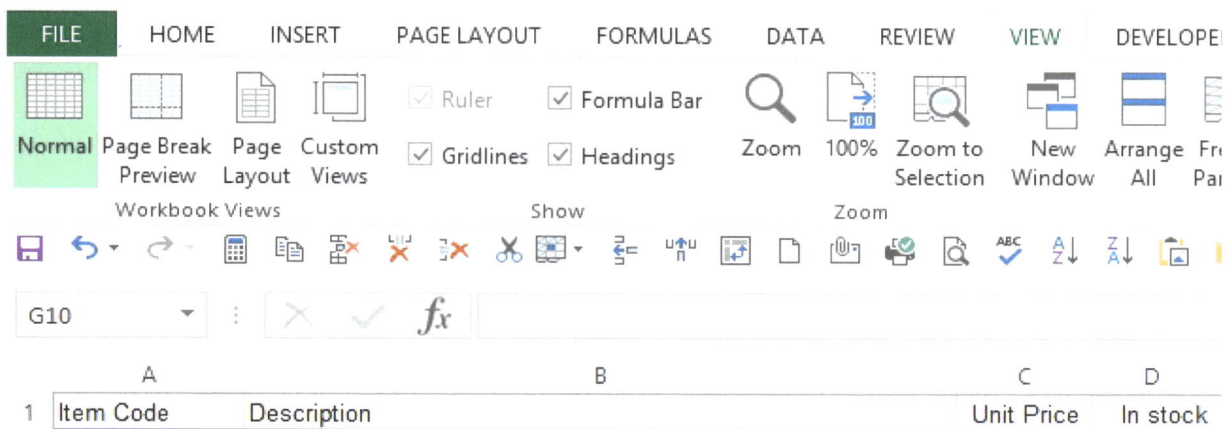

Fig. 92

Now fill in the worksheet from cell A2 – D25 as shown in fig. 93.

	A	B	C	D
1	Item Code	Description	Unit Price	In stock
2	SERV001	Server 2012	£4,538.80	5
3	ACE001	Acer Aspire E5-571 15.6" laptop	£ 411.00	10
4	ACE002	Acer Aspire E1-570 15.6" laptop	£ 385.99	15
5	SSN001	Samsung ATIV Book 4 15.6" Notebook	£ 449.00	9
6	SSN002	Samsung 530 U3C 13.3 inc ultrabook	£ 699.99	6
7	SSN003	Samsung Chromebook XE 303c12-A	£ 229.00	9
8	LEN001	Lenovo G50 - 70 15.6 inch Notebook	£ 379.00	5
9	LEN002	Lenovo S20-30 11.6 inch Touchscreen	£ 270.00	8
10	DEL001	Dell Inspiron 3531 loaptop	£ 300.00	7
11	DEL002	Dell Latitude E4310	£ 350.00	12
12	APL001	Apple 13 inch MacBook Pro	£ 999.00	20
13	APL002	Apple MacBook 15.4" laptop (intel core i7 2.2 GH, 16GB RAM	£1,599.00	15
14	KIN001	Kindle Fire HDX 8.9" HDX Display WIFI	£ 329.00	17
15	SST001	Samsung Galaxy Tab 4.10 inch Tablet (Black)	£ 294.56	10
16	SST002	Samsung Galaxy Tab S 10.5" Titanium Bronze Tablet	£ 322.00	11
17	API001	Apple ipad Air 2 16GB WIFI space grey	£ 349.00	30
18	API002	Apple ipad mini (7.9 inch multi - touch) Tablet PC 32GB WIFI	£ 425.25	13
19	CAN001	Canon EOS Digital SLR Camera (EF-S 18.55 cm f/3.5)	£ 749.00	15
20	CAN002	Canon Poershot SX700 HS Zoom	£ 320.00	25
21	CAN003	Canon SX60 HS Power shot Digital Camera	£ 429.65	22
22	NIK001	Nikon D3200 Digital SLR Camera with 18.55mm VR lens kit	£ 649.99	7
23	NIK002	Nikon D5000 Digital SLR Camera with 18-55 mm VR lens kit	£ 499.99	9
24	PAN001	Panasonic PTA 6000E LCD projector - 3D	£1,999.00	3
25	LG001	LGPA70G Portable WXGALED Projector	£ 514.80	5
26	EPS001	Epson EH-TW5100 Full HD 1080p 3D Home cinema & gaming	£ 615.25	7
27	LG002	LGPF80G Full HD LED projector	£1,078.80	8
28	BEN001	BenQ W1200 DLP Projector	£ 736.38	5
29	VIE001	Viewsonic PLED-W800 DLP Projector	£ 495.67	9

Fig. 93

Now, select the data range from A2-D29 and name it Product. Type the word Product to replace the text A2 in the area shown by a green tick in fig. 94.

Product ✓	:	× ✓ fx	SERV001		

	A	B	C	D
2	SERV001	Server 2012	£4,538.80	5
3	ACE001	Acer Aspire E5-571 15.6" laptop	£ 411.00	10
4	ACE002	Acer Aspire E1-570 15.6" laptop	£ 385.99	15
5	SSN001	Samsung ATIV Book 4 15.6" Notebook	£ 449.00	9
6	SSN002	Samsung 530 U3C 13.3 inc ultrabook	£ 699.99	6
7	SSN003	Samsung Chromebook XE 303c12-A	£ 229.00	9
8	LEN001	Lenovo G50 – 70 15.6 inch Notebook	£ 379.00	5
9	LEN002	Lenovo S20-30 11.6 inch Touchscreen	£ 270.00	8
10	DEL001	Dell Inspiron 3531 loaptop	£ 300.00	7
11	DEL002	Dell Latitude E4310	£ 350.00	12
12	APL001	Apple 13 inch MacBook Pro	£ 999.00	20
13	APL002	Apple MacBook 15.4" laptop (intel core i7 2.2 GH, 16GB RAM	£1,599.00	15
14	KIN001	Kindle Fire HDX 8.9" HDX Display WIFI	£ 329.00	17
15	SST001	Samsung Galaxy Tab 4.10 inch Tablet (Black)	£ 294.56	10
16	SST002	Samsung Galaxy Tab S 10.5" Titanium Bronze Tablet	£ 322.00	11
17	API001	Apple ipad Air 2 16GB WIFI space grey	£ 349.00	30
18	API002	Apple ipad mini (7.9 inch multi - touch) Tablet PC 32GB WIFI	£ 425.25	13
19	CAN001	Canon EOS Digital SLR Camera (EF–S 18.55 cm f/3.5)	£ 749.00	15
20	CAN002	Canon Poershot SX700 HS Zoom	£ 320.00	25
21	CAN003	Canon SX60 HS Power shot Digital Camera	£ 429.65	22
22	NIK001	Nikon D3200 Digital SLR Camera with 18.55mm VR lens kit	£ 649.99	7
23	NIK002	Nikon D5000 Digital SLR Camera with 18-55 mm VR lens kit	£ 499.99	9
24	PAN001	Panasonic PTA 6000E LCD projector – 3D	£1,999.00	3
25	LG001	LGPA70G Portable WXGALED Projector	£ 514.80	5
26	EPS001	Epson EH-TW5100 Full HD 1080p 3D Home cinema & gaming	£ 615.25	7
27	LG002	LGPF80G Full HD LED projector	£1,078.80	8
28	BEN001	BenQ W1200 DLP Projector	£ 736.38	5
29	VIE001	Viewsonic PLED-W800 DLP Projector	£ 495.67	9

Fig. 94

Okay,

Open another new worksheet in the same workbook (name it Customer List) and write down the following list of customers.

Here is how it should look like in your excel sheet when you are done - see fig. 95.

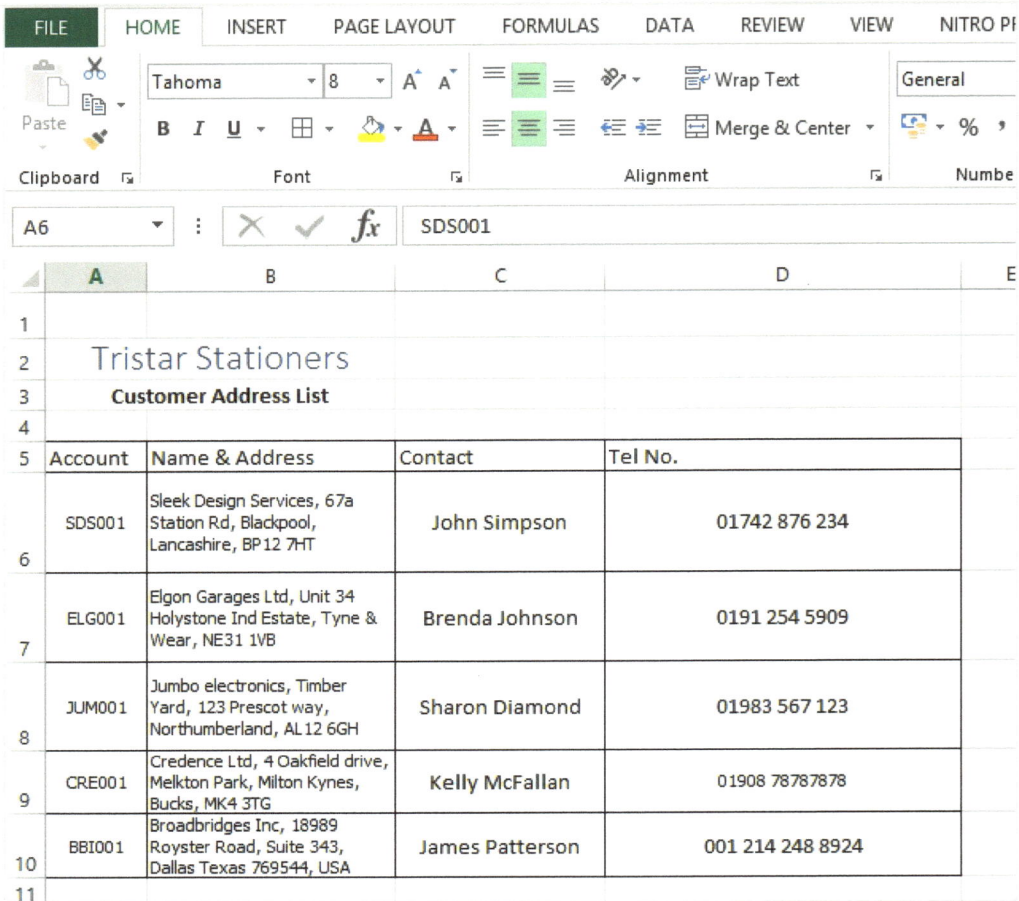

Fig. 95

Now highlight cell A6-D10 and name that range Customer. We will use it later.

Using the VLOOKUP formula/function

Okay,

In order to test the VLOOKUP formula we're about to write, we first enter a valid item code into cell A11 of the blank invoice template we created earlier on.

Fig. 96

Next, we move the active cell to the cell in which we want information retrieved from the database by VLOOKUP to be stored. Interestingly, this is the step that most people get wrong. To explain further: We are about to create a VLOOKUP formula that will retrieve the description that corresponds to the item code in cell A11. Where do we want this description put when we get it? In cell B11, of course. So that's where we write the VLOOKUP formula – in cell B11.

Select cell B11.

We need to locate the VLOOKUP function and get some assistance in completing it. Follow steps 1-3 as illustrated in the figure below.

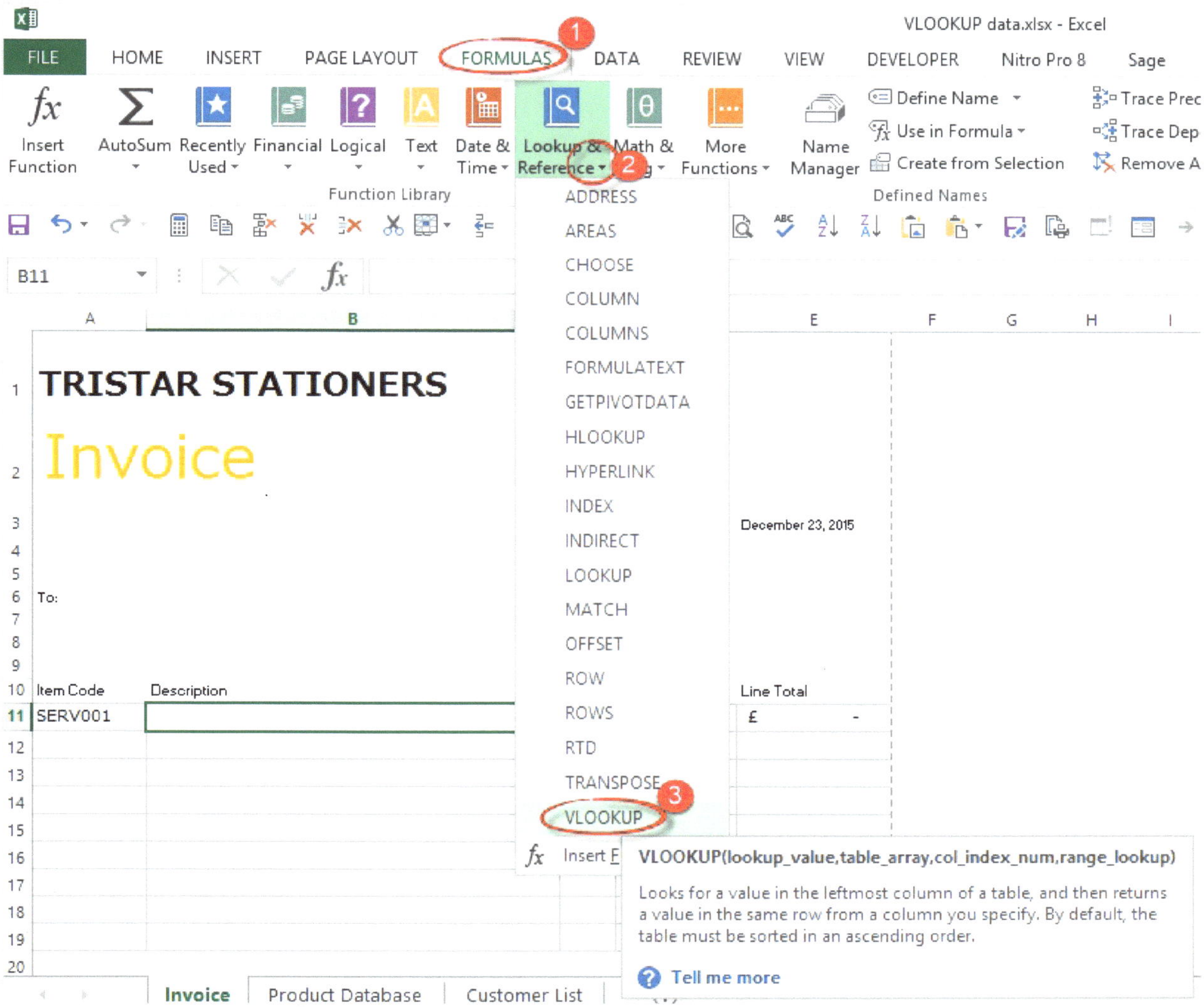

Fig. 97

VLOOKUP Function Arguments

After step 3 as illustrated in the figure above, The Function Arguments box appears, prompting us for all the arguments (or parameters) needed in order to complete the VLOOKUP function. You can think of this box as the function is asking us the following questions:

1. *What unique identifier are you looking up in the database?*

2. *Where is the database?*

3. *Which piece of information from the database, associated with the unique identifier, do you wish to have retrieved for you?*

The first three arguments are shown in bold, indicating that they are mandatory arguments (the VLOOKUP function is incomplete without them and will not return a valid value). The fourth argument is not bold, meaning that it's optional.

See figure below.

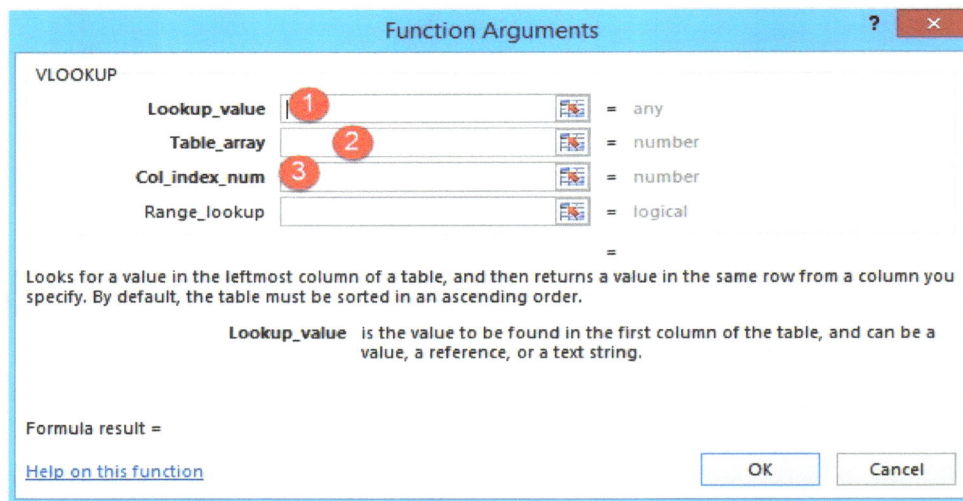

Fig. 98

We will complete the arguments in order, top to bottom.

The first argument we need to complete is the Lookup value argument. The function needs us to tell it where to find the unique identifier (the item code in this case) that it should be retuning the description of. We must select the item code we entered earlier (in A11).

Click on the selector icon to the right of the first argument.

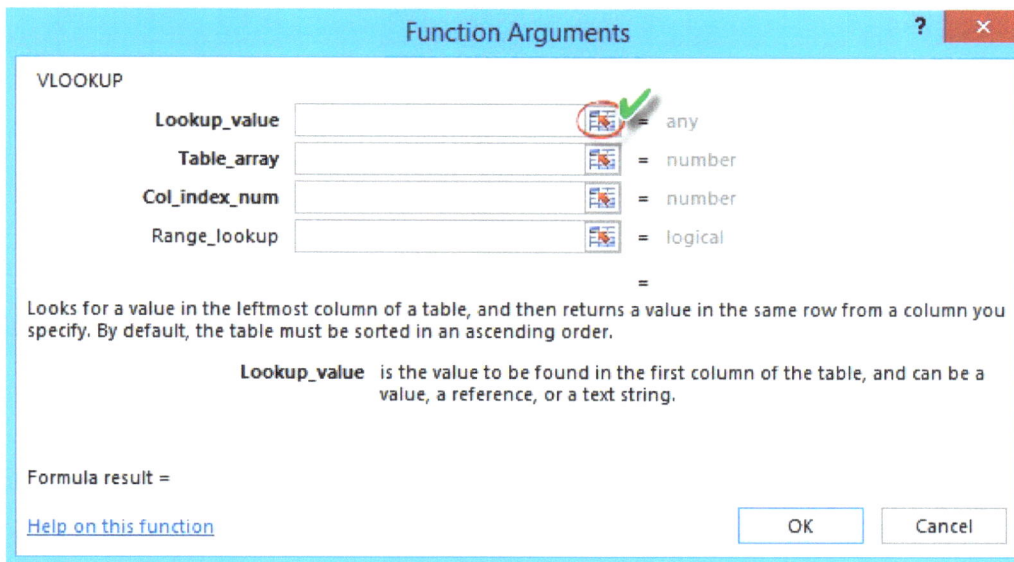

Fig. 99

Then click once on the cell containing the item code (A11), and press Enter.

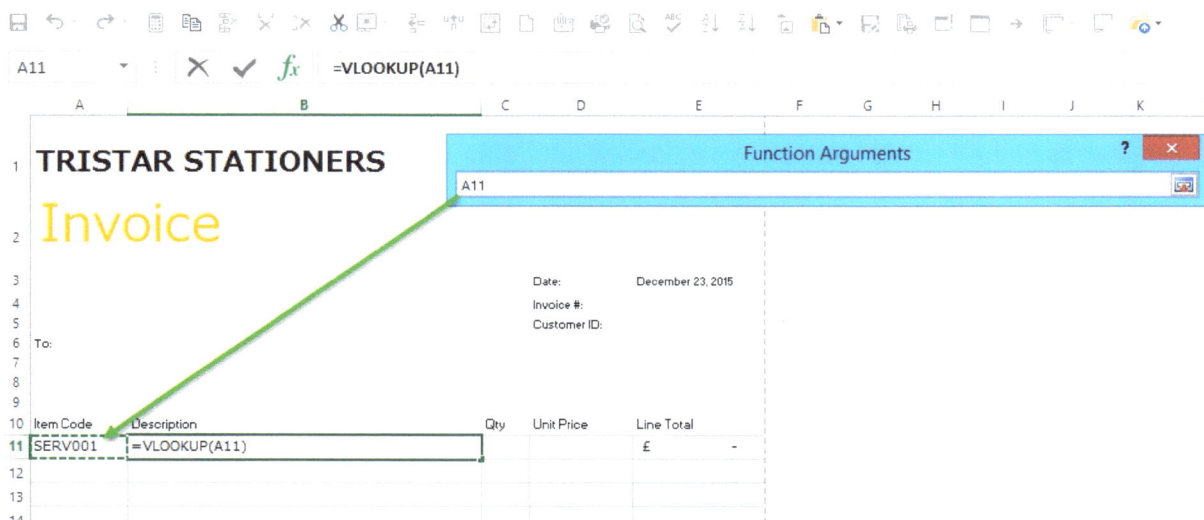

Fig. 100

The value of "A11" is inserted into the first argument.

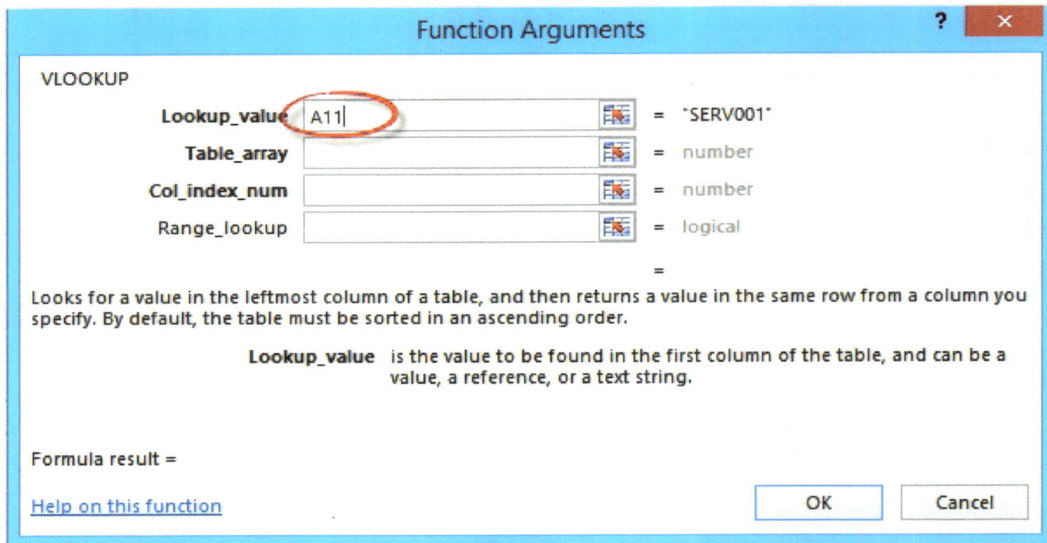

Fig. 101

Now we need to enter a value for the Table_array argument. In other words, we need to tell VLOOKUP where to find the database/list. Click on the Table _array box and type in Product (Do you remember we named the Product database range – Product? that is why we are typing the word Product here). We are basically telling VLOOKUP that the database is called product.

See figure below.

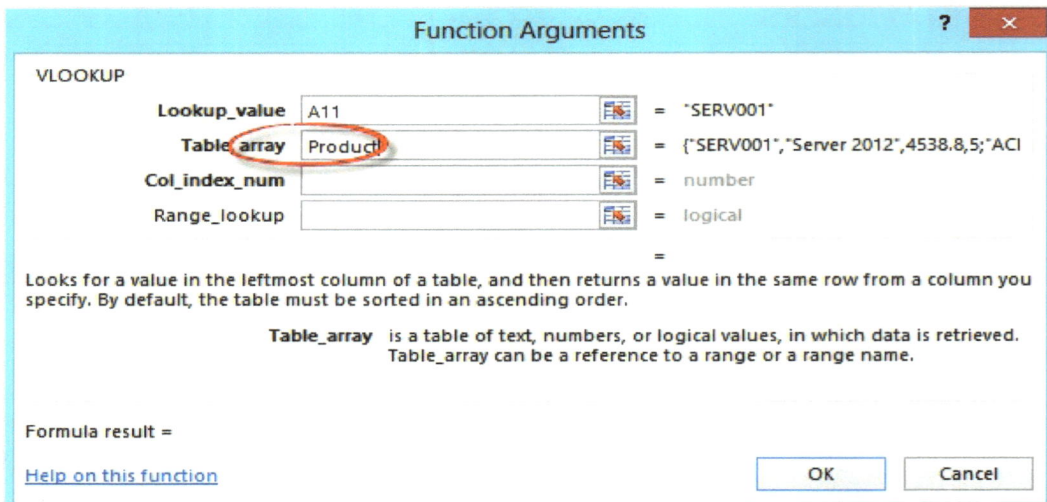

Fig. 102

Now we need to enter the third argument, Col_index_num. We use this argument to specify to VLOOKUP which piece of information from the database, associate with our item code in A11, we wish to have returned to us. In this particular example, we wish to have the item's description returned to us. If you look on the database worksheet, you'll notice that the "Description" column is the second column in the database. This means that we must enter a value of "2" into the Col_index_num box: see figure below.

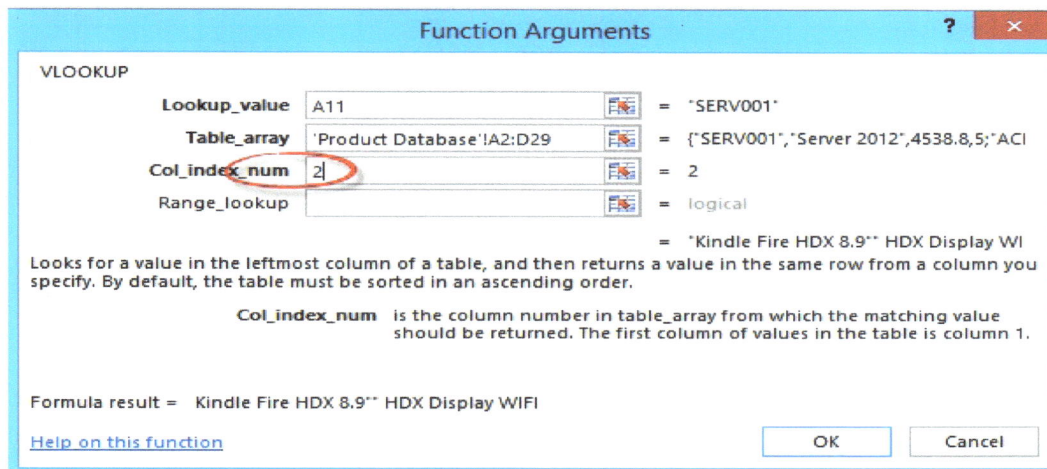

Fig. 103

It is important to note that that we are not entering a "2" here because the "Description" column is in the B column on that worksheet. If the database happened to start in column K of the worksheet, we would still enter a "2" in this field.

Finally, we need to decide whether to enter a value into the final VLOOKUP argument, Range_lookup. This argument requires either a true or false value, or it should be left blank. When using VLOOKUP with databases (as is true 90% of the time), then the way to decide what to put in this argument can be thought of as follows:

If the first column of the database (the column that contains the unique identifiers) is sorted alphabetically/numerically in ascending order, then it's possible to enter a value of true into this argument, or leave it blank.

If the first column of the database is not sorted, or it's sorted in descending order, then you must enter a value of false into this argument.

As the first column of our database is not sorted, we enter false into this argument.

That's it! We've entered all the information required for VLOOKUP to return the value we need. Click the OK button.

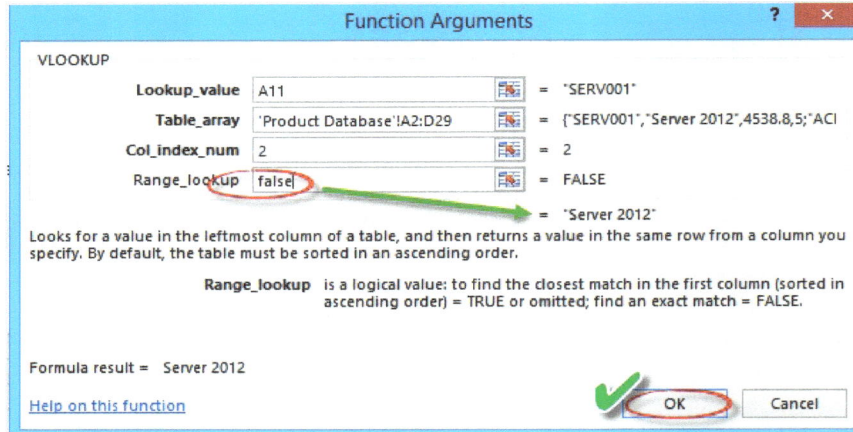

Fig. 104

Notice that after you click OK as illustrated in the figure above, the description corresponding to item code "SERV001" has been correctly entered into cell B11 (illustrated by letter "A" in the figure below of which the full VLOOKUP formula is illustrated by letter "B" in the figure below).

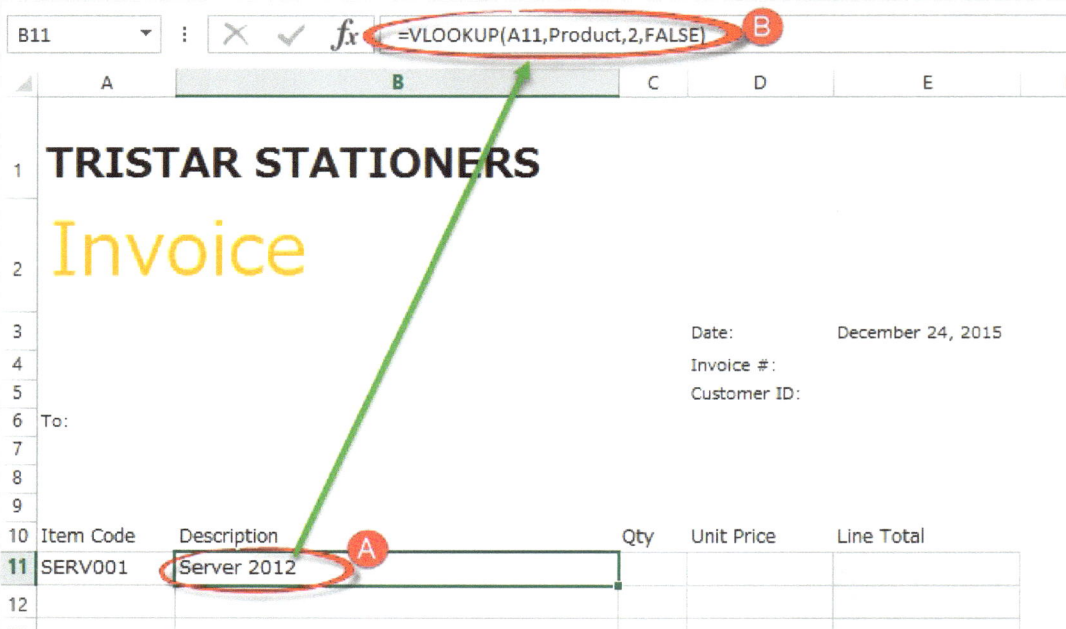

Fig. 105

We can perform a similar set of steps to get the item's price returned into cell D11. Note that the new formula must be created in cell D11. The result will look like this:

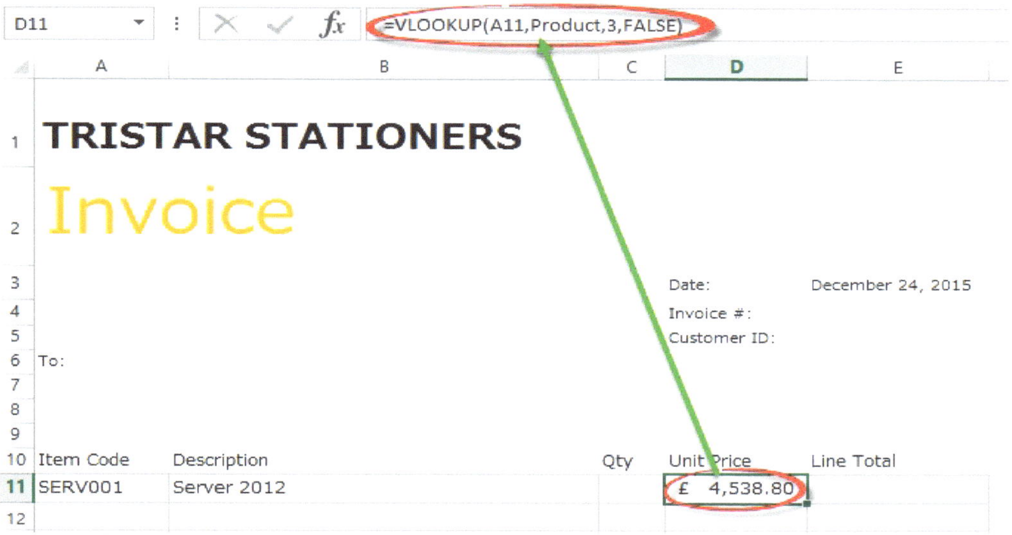

Fig. 106

Use the "ISBLANK" and "IF" function in cells B11 & D1. This is to avaid the #N/A signs in cell B11 & D11 should there be no value in A11.

Here is how the formulas should look like;

B11-=IF(ISBLANK(A11),"",VLOOKUP(A11,2,FALSE))or=IF(A11="","",VLOOKUP(A11,2,FALSE))

D11-=IF(ISBLANK(A11),"",VLOOKUP(A11,3,FALSE))or=IF(A11="","",VLOOKUP(A11,3,FALSE))

Note that the only difference between the two formulas is that the third argument (Col_index_num) has changed from a "2" to a "3" for formula in D11 (because we want data retrieved from the 3rd column in the database for the case of the unit price of the product code in A11).

Now copy the formula in B11 to B12-B19. To do this select cell B11, then hoover the mouse at the bottom right corner of cell B11 till you see the dark + , once you see it, click and hold at the bottom right side of cell B11 and drag your mouse down to cell B19 then release it.

Do the same for formula in D11.

See fig. 107.

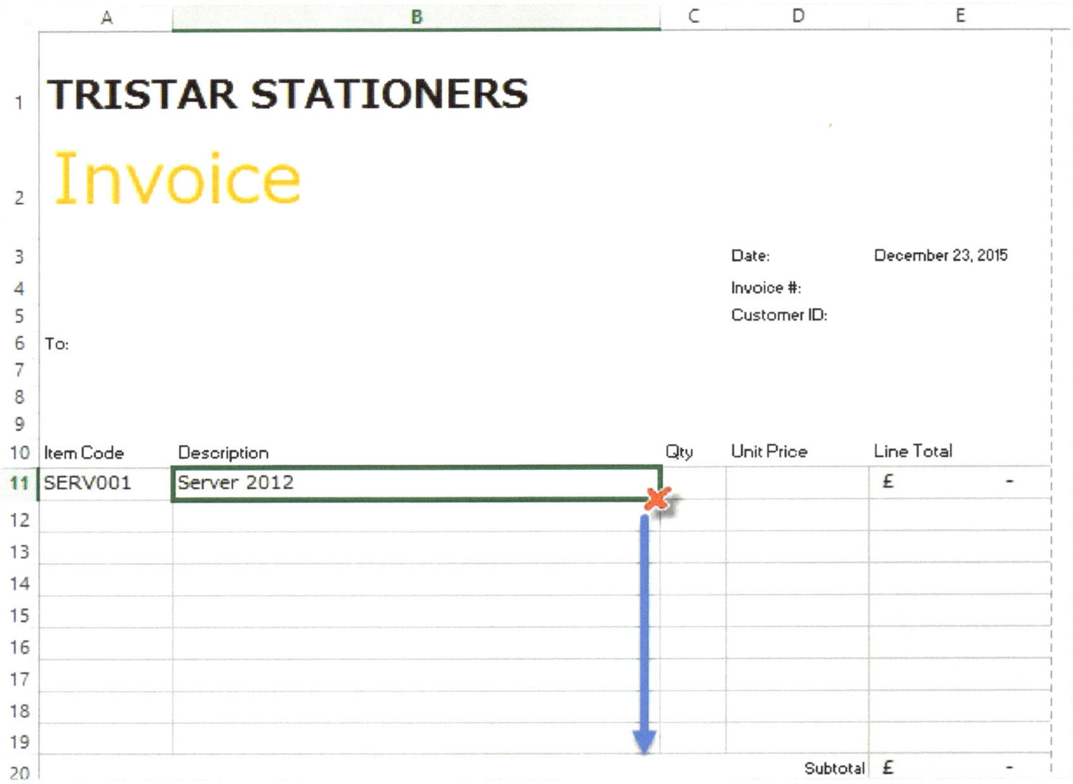

Fig. 107

Now, if we enter a different item code into cell A11, we will begin to see the power of the VLOOKUP function: The description cell changes to match the new item code.

First, let's put a drop down list for all the products into cell A11 – A19. To do this, left click to select cell A11, then hold the click and drag your mouse down until you reach cell A19, then release the click – You have now selected cell A11-A19.

Incorporating Data Validation

Select Data>Data validation>Data Validation again. See figure below.

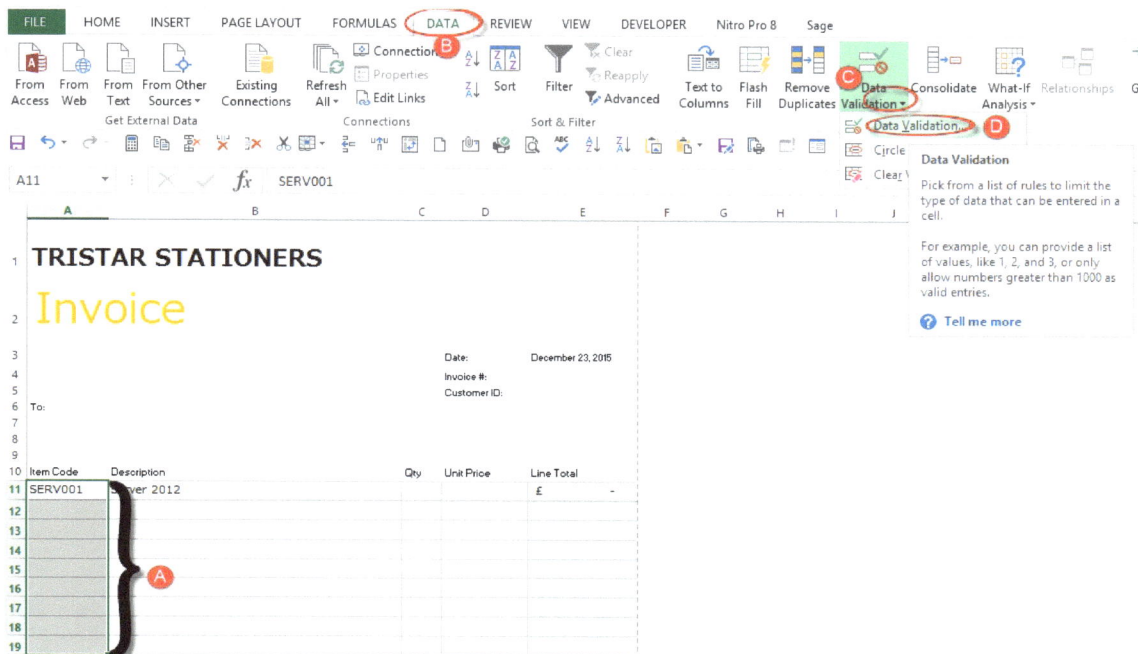

Fig. 108

Once you select Data validation (step D as illustrated in the figure above) a window similar to the figure below will appear.

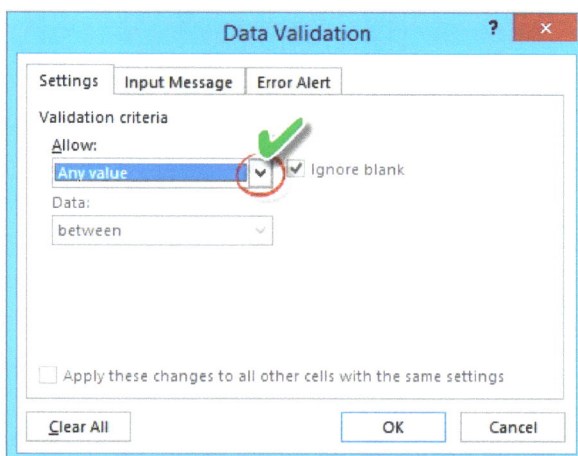

Fig. 109

Click on the drop down arrow and select "List".

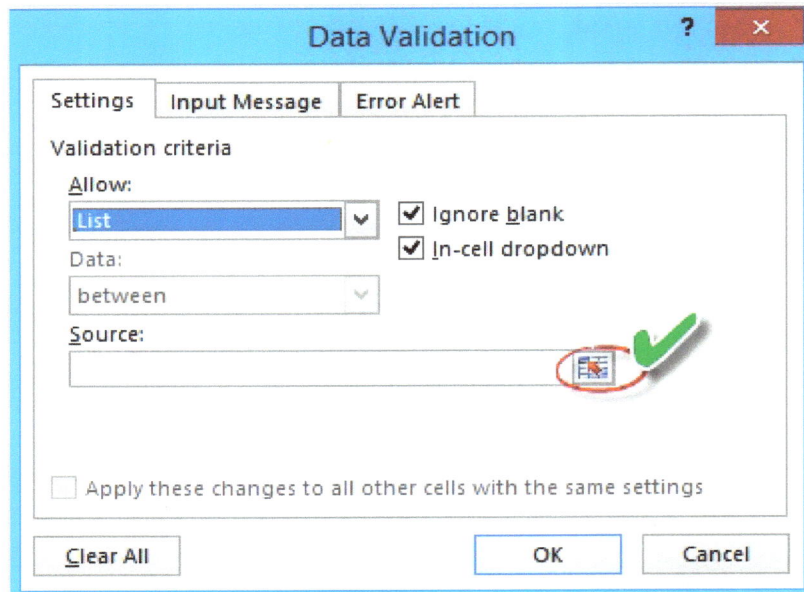

Fig. 110

Now click on the selector icon to the right of source then select the product database sheet and then select cell A2 – A29 and press Enter. See figure below.

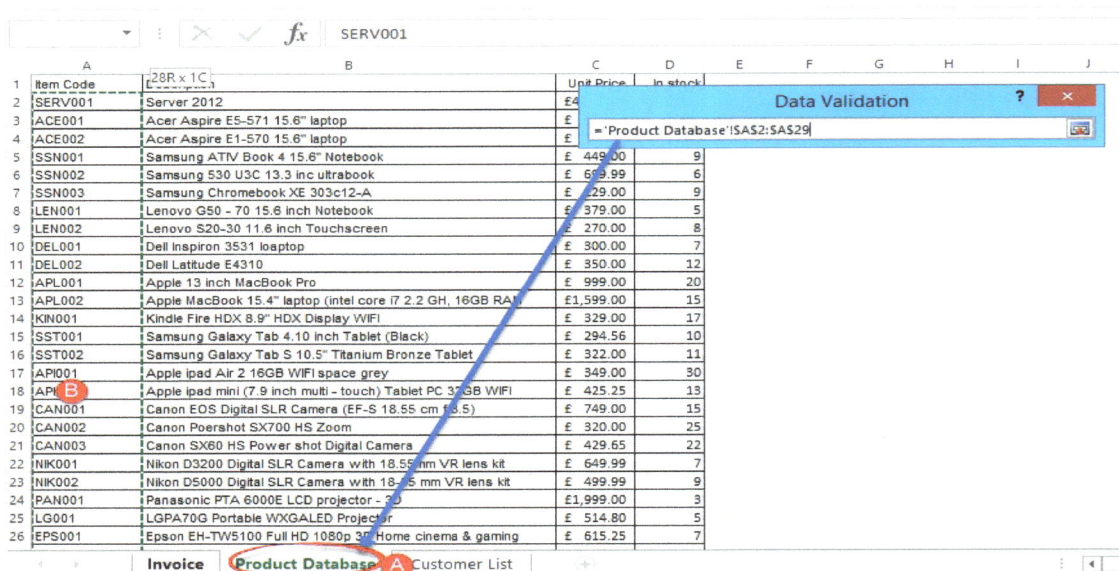

Fig. 111

After you press Enter, this is what you will see;

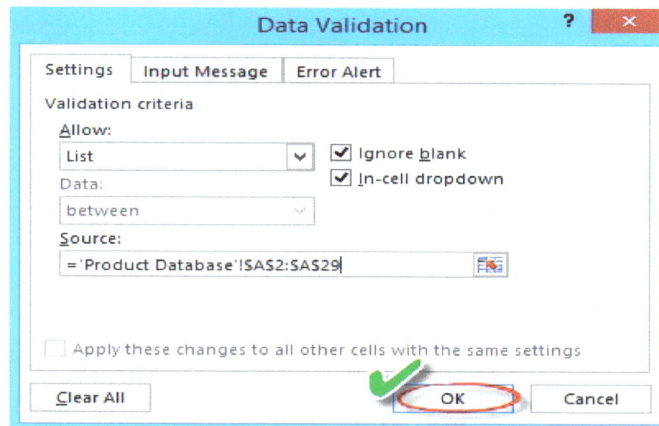

Fig. 112

Click OK,

You can now select any of the product codes from cell A11 – A19, see below illustrated by drop down arrow in "A" and products in "B".

Fig. 113

Let's complete this invoice template by automating the input of the customer details once a customer account is selected.

Put a data validation for customer account numbers in cell E5.

Merge cells B6-B8, select the merged cell and click "Wrap Text", "Align left" and "Middle Align" – see figure below.

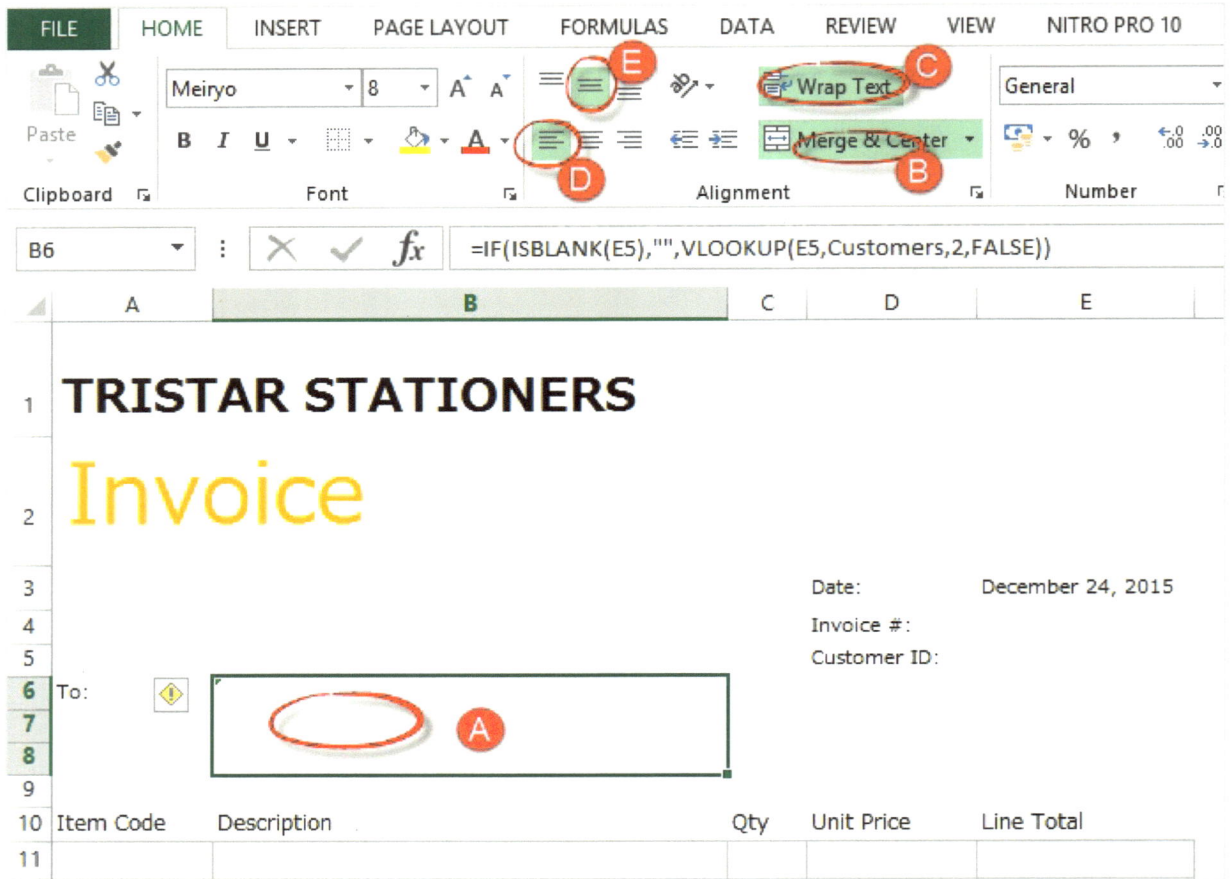

Fig. 114

Now put a VLOOKUP formula to the merged cells to return the customer address selected in cell E5.

Here is how the VLOOKUP function will look like.

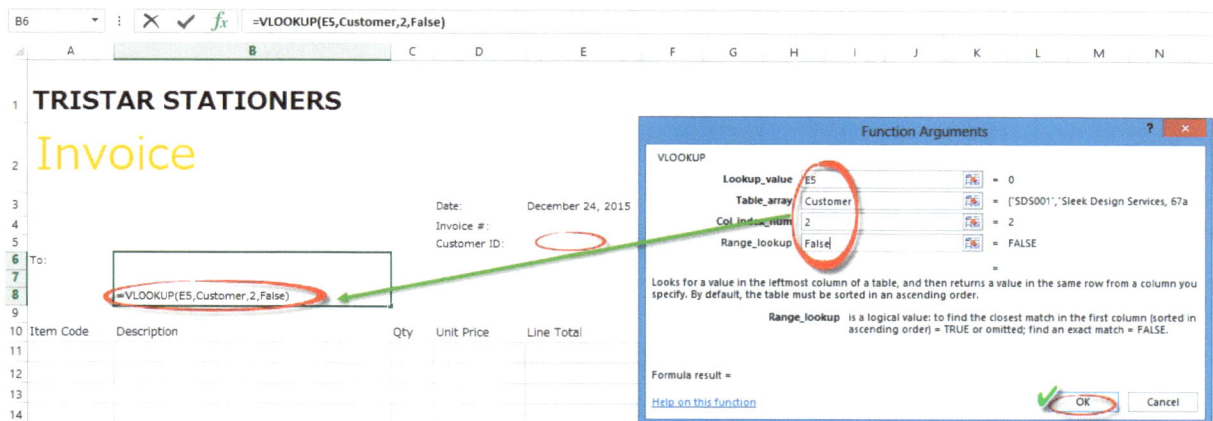

Fig. 115

Use "ISBLANK" and "IF" function as well in the merged cell to avoid #N/A error in case there is no value in cell E5. So the formula should look like this; =IF(ISBLANK(E5),"" ,VLOOKUP(E5,Customer,2,False)) or =IF(E5="", "",VLOOKUP(E5,Customer,2,False)). Click on the merged cell B6-B8 and on the formula bar include the missing "IF" & "ISBLANK" function parts to VLOOKUP formula.

Fig. 116

Now let's test our work! I am quite excited now, wow!

Okay,

Here is a purchase order you have received from one of your customers;

Sleek Design Services

Purchase Order

Date: 24-Dec-15
PO # [100]

Supplier		Deliver To	
	Sales Manager		John Simpson
	Tristar Stationers		Sleek Design Services
	55 Shelton Street		67a Station Road Blackpool
	London, WC2H 9JQ		Lancashire, BP12 7HT
	020 7836 1234		01742876234

Shipping Method	Shipping Terms	Delivery Date
Standard	As per agreement	No later than 15 Jan 2016

Qty	Description	Unit Price	Line Total
1	Server 2012	£4,538.80	£4,538.80
5	Kindle Fire HDX 8.9" HDX Display WIFI	£329.00	£1,645.00
		Subtotal	£6,183.80
		Sales Tax@ 20%	£1,236.76
		Total	£7,420.56

Please send two copies of your invoice.

Enter this order in accordance with the prices, terms, delivery method, and specifications listed above.

Please notify us immediately if you are unable to ship as specified.

Send all correspondence to:

John Simpson
67a Station Road, Blackpool
Lancashire, BP12 7HT
Phone 0174286234
Fax 01742876000

Authorized by   Date

Automating tasks using VLOOKUP function

Now, let's raise an invoice for this customer using the invoice template you have just created using the VLOOKUP function. Make it invoice number 1234.

Select cell E5 (notice that you will see a drop down arrow) and select from the drop down list account code SDS001. Notice that the name and address of the customer appears on merged cells B6-B8 once you select the account code in cell E5.

Now select cell A11 and notice that a drop down arrow becomes visible. Click the drop down arrow and from the drop down list select SERV001 which is the code for the Server 2012. Notice that the product description- Server 2012 is automatically displayed on cell B11 and the unit price is automatically displayed on cell D11. Type in 1 on cell C11.

Select cell A12 and via the drop down list, select KIN001 and notice that in cell B12, "Kindle Fire HDX 8.9' Display WIFI" is automatically appears because of the VLOOKUP formula in Cell B12. Also notice that in cell D12 the price of £329.00 is automatically displayed because yet again, you have the VLOOKUP formula in cell D12.

And because the customer needs 5 of the Kindle Fire HDX, type in 5 in cell C12.

Here is how the final invoice looks like now:

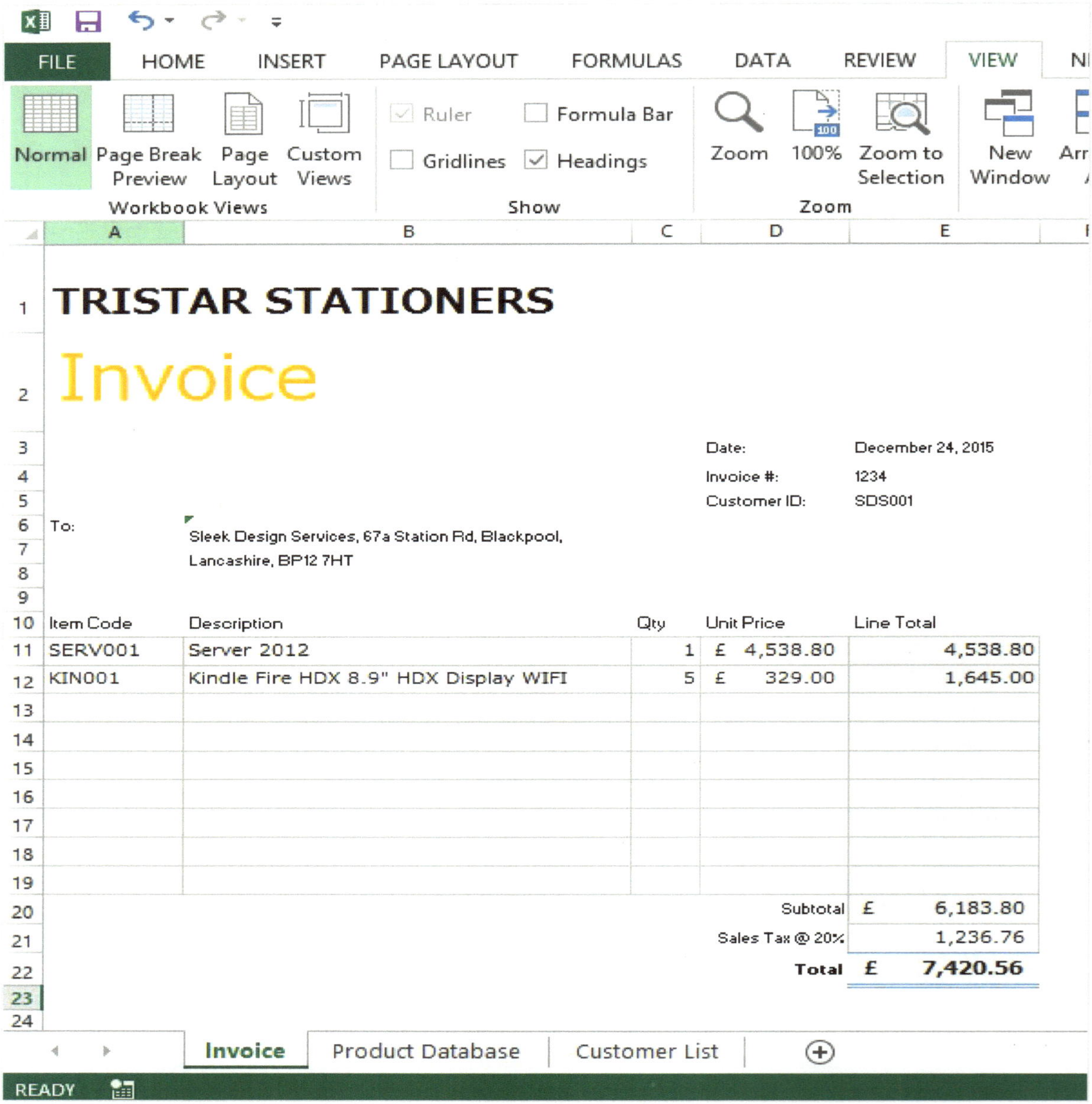

Fig. 117

There you have it! VLOOKUP, done!

I hope you enjoyed that. I certainly did.

A smile is my style

OTHER BOOKS BY STERLING LIBS

S NO.	BOOK TITLE
1	**THE TRAINEE ACCOUNTANT** - How to have a successful accounting career
2	**MONTH END ACCOUNTING PROCEDURES** - Detailed step by step guide
3	**THE ACCOUNTS ASSISTANT JOB MANUAL** - How to do the regular day to day tasks of an accounts assistant
4	**THE WAY TO GET AN ACCOUNTING JOB IN THE UK** - The 5 Strategic steps
5	**GET YOUR VAT RETURN DONE IN 5 STEPS**
6	**BUSINESS INTELLIGENCE** - Start, Build & Run your own business and become financially independent
7	**FINANCIAL ACCOUNTING** - UK Proctical Work Experience.
8	**HOW TO PRODUCE MANAGEMENT ACCOUNTING REPORTS –** Cash Flow Forecast, Profit & Loss, Budgets & variance analysis, break-even, KPI analysis. Work Experience guide.
9	**ADVANCED EXCEL -** How to Use VLOOKUP & INDEX MATCH Functions
10	**HOW TO FILE ACCOUNTS & ANNUAL RETURN TO HMRC & COMPANIES' HOUSE** - Detailed step by step practical experience guide for Accountants.
11	**PIVOT TABLES PRACTICAL EXPERIENCE GUIDE** – Pivot tables simply & beautifully illustrated with screenshots. Accountants Edition.

HOW TO GET THESE BOOKS

1. Go to www.sterlinglibs.com or

2. Go to amazon.co.uk

3. Type in Sterling Libs at the search bar in amazon.co.uk website

4. You will see all of the above books

5. Select the one(s) you like & proceed to check out

www.ingramcontent.com/pod-product-compliance
Lightning Source LLC
Chambersburg PA
CBHW041730210326
41598CB00008B/832